THE JOURNEY OF A LIFETIME

For Entrants to the Corporate World & SMEs

PARAM BHARGAVA, Ph.D.

AUTHOR OF BREAK FREE AND GROW

ISBN
Hardcase 979-8-89632-740-0
Paperback 979-8-89632-354-9

Dedication

My grandson, Anant (5 years old), asked what I used to do besides writing and reading books. I said, "I cannot answer in the next ten minutes, but I will write for you so that you can learn as you grow." Thus, this book is dedicated to Anant who always has a question - WHY.

Contents

Note: The names of the individuals referenced in this book have been intentionally changed to ensure their privacy

Foreword

It has been my pleasure to know Dr. Param Bhargava since my joining of ICI India in 1972. Our relationship has grown from mere acquaintance to a strong professional association when Param became the head of the Paints business of ICI India and I became CFO in the '90s. I always admired his strategic thinking ,single minded focus on results and the way he could build a strong team as a coach rather than a senior, to turn around the business in a short time.

I find this book 'The Journey of a lifetime' to be very useful for young managers who need to know what it takes to grow in a corporate environment. There are adequate inputs that can help readers appreciate the importance of innovativeness, strategic thinking, planning, managing people, and their mindset. Once the readers of this book fully understand and practice these attributes, they will enjoy their work and succeed in their workplaces.

Dr. Param Bhargava started his career in research, which was his specialisation. Over a period of self-learning, he smoothly moved to other areas and ultimately became a successful business leader as Regional Director (refinish paints) of ICI Asia Pacific, Singapore. The fact that he was successful in dealing with different types of businesses and in different organisations shows that he learnt various management principles which have been elaborated in this book. Param, through this book, has shared his professional experiences in dealing successfully with different challenges he faced in his long career in multiple countries and organisations. These are elegantly explained, and Param has supported the use of these management tools.

I take this opportunity to thank Dr. Param Bhargava for his efforts in writing this book for the benefit of young managers in the corporate world and SMEs.

– M R Rajaram
Former Director and CFO of Akzo Nobel India Ltd.

Introduction

Search for a purpose.

If you do not have a purpose, life feels empty and wanders without a purpose. The need for achieving something worthwhile, a 'meaning', is ever present in our subconscious mind and plays up very often.

Peter Drucker said-

'Our mission in life is to make a positive difference, and not to prove how smart or right we are'

We all need to identify a goal in life which, when followed through in that direction, gives us inner satisfaction. When we have a goal, we work around to make it happen and do not wait for things to happen. We do it regardless of the constraints we face because it defines who you are. As we progress, it provides partial satisfaction, happiness, and motivation to continue with high energy.

If we are after the short-lived pleasures of the senses, it provides short-lived happiness. One has to search for a deeper meaning or a purpose to motivate at different stages of life. This objective does not necessarily need to come from heredity, environment, school, or society but from your internal churn. This objective brings in a higher degree of self-discipline and stronger commitment, resulting in self-improvement.

Out of these, self-discipline is the starting point for accomplishing your medium- and long-term goals and is described later in detail.

Self-Discovery

In order to know who we are - we need to go through a process of self-discovery and conclude what values and principles will be our compass of life. It is the 'WHY' - the purpose the enterprise exists. Why do we want to do what we want to do? This debate at the top is critical to bring clarity to the vision, values, and goals.

It is important to establish a vision and set of values by which an individual or enterprise will be guided. If one is not clear what their own values are, how can one set goals for the short term and possibly for the long-term?

During my teens, the internal need was to realise an ideal that would make a difference in my chosen area of expertise. The goal was fuzzy but gradually became clearer with internal debate over time.

We are successful when we come to be aware of who we are, what we care about, why we do, and what we do. The growth journey of life depends on how well we understand ourselves, what we value, and why we value it. In the end, we need to develop an internal compass - "Inner self" to guide us through the maze of life.

Controlling the mind is the biggest challenge we have. If left alone, the mind has a habit of wandering. Normally, it processes negative thoughts more often than positive ones. Thus, with better control of the mind, we can improve our life. You have a choice to think about what you would like to think. Life depends on our thoughts running through our minds continuously. Our life depends on the quality of thoughts we have, and thus it is up to us to think about what we want to be in life. It is said that -

'We become to what we think most of the time.'

– Earl Nightingale - Author

The thinking process involves:

1. Process information.
2. Develop options.
3. Weigh the few options and decide on the best one.
4. Identify what problems one is likely to encounter during the implementation and what could be possible solutions.
5. Cultivate a growth mindset and act accordingly.

It covers various cognitive functions such as perception, memory, attention, and reasoning, etc. It has an impact on mental and physical health. Our thoughts shape our behaviours and actions, which are crucial in today's world. So, to be successful in life, one has to be good at managing the thoughts passing through our minds.

It is felt that we all change with time, but core personality traits, as are passions and interests, remain steady throughout adulthood. Research indicates that very early signs of personality and behaviour could be visible at the age of three to five, and these traits were demonstrable even at the age of twenty-six. This is likely due to our inheritance and the environment in which we spent those formative years.

Some of us might have certain disadvantages for opportunities compared to individuals from well-to-do families. Individuals with a disadvantage will have to work harder and have no place for error at work.

We were segregated very early in life as talented vs. average. Many schools treat the so-called 'talented' differently than the average. The usual words used to extrapolate progress in life were how talented one is and how passionate one is about their choices, the decision-making process, self-control, and empathy.

Though talent is described as a natural way of behaving and thinking, investment of time is important because if you have talent and do not work on it, your chances of success are low. The most successful people possess talent and work hard to actualise it.

Each advises finding your passion so that you are better than others in that selected field. While traits are seeded by the age of 3-5, a real understanding of self emerges in the early twenties. Around that time, traits/competencies are displayed and can be estimated, leading to a career path.

This book has three parts:

1. My learning and experience of ICI days, PPG, the largest paints manufacturer in the world as Regional Director, Asia, located in KL, as MD Perstorp India, a Sweden-based chemical company, India - Consultant Hempel, a Danish paints unit, and Dulux of Australia enabled me to write about such enriched experiences.
2. Application of my knowledge with SMEs in India.
3. Application of certain concepts that are highly applicable to an ambitious student of management and can be used by anybody who is on the journey of mastering something new in life.

I have described some of my experiences, and some of these traits will be visible to the reader while they read the book and can relate to some of their own experiences.

My belief was, once you have decided on a goal after evaluating all the possible downsides, you should fully commit and break up the task into micro-actions and work hard to make them happen. We have stressed goal setting adequately later in Chapter 11.

Goals can be modified, if necessary, at different stages of life, or the first one may be suitable throughout the journey.

Self-discipline is crucial to manage the task ahead of time and persevere until achieved. Life is full of challenges.

Once achieved, let it go and move on to the next challenge.

With this exposure, the author's life journey started, and I tried to follow this concept to the extent possible throughout my life as a guiding principle. This book is about the journey of my life. There is nothing unusual but describes a roadmap, with its challenges faced and processes used to overcome them and keep learning by your own self for a higher level of being.

Learning from this experience can be of value for individuals who are entering the higher education field or candidates preparing for their first job or moving from one job to another. My life faced a lot of challenges; my approach was to select the right goal and the right process to resolve this and not worry too much about the outcome. The fact is if the process is right, the outcome has to be right. There are minor setbacks that also need to be addressed along the way. Another major factor that we ignore at times is the people. One has to have the right people to build a highly successful enterprise.

Every life has its ups and downs, and a growth mindset knows how to succeed in not-so-good times and good times.

Part One

Chapter-1

Dream Stage

I came from a striving middle class background. My father was a revenue officer in the Government, and his assignments were for 2-3 years in one location. The family moved along with him every 2-3 years, and I was admitted to a new local school each time he moved.

My parents had advised me to be friendly with new groups and differentiate between good and not-so-good friends. Stay with good friends most of the time and learn good habits, e.g. timekeeping, completion of homework on time, being in class on time, etc. My learning, in a way, started from that age. There were many studious children who were either reluctant to express themselves or were introverted. What I had figured out was that learning alone was inadequate till you convert those learnings into practice. It was a slow process to inculcate in your behaviour but if you are determined, it would gradually take shape. Since I was always catching up on the course work being new in school, I had to learn to ask questions even though at times they were simple and cynical in the eyes of other classmates. Gradually, I also developed the ability to ask critical questions and what you need to resolve with the help of friends or your own self. This 'critical information seeking differentiation' was the result of this experience.

A simple guideline that emerged was to be respectful, and a behaviour acceptable to the environment in which one was operating. I had realised, in a small measure, the importance of empathy, honesty, learning and hard work as crucial for growth in life. Also, to attend pending tasks before time and do not defer learnings to some future date. At this stage, the internal need was to be self-disciplined to achieve something different, which was worthwhile. The goal was getting clearer as time passed.

*To search for purpose requires self-reflection and self–knowledge. Each of us has different strengths, talents, insights and experiences that shape who we are. Thus, we all will have different goals which fit into who we are and what we value. It not only involves the person but also where we come from, where we are going and how we fit into the environment. Researchers at Texas A&M University have found a relationship between identity and purpose; knowing oneself is a predictor of meaning in life. (1)

At age 16, I had gone to earn my graduate degree at Pilani. Major changes got initiated, primarily in the process of **learning***(*competencies used are explained in Chapter 14) and development of different competencies needed to succeed.

Competency relates to how quickly one can learn, understand, and apply to the new role and how open one is to implementing those new ideas.

In the following description, every block activity was perceived as a life cycle. These life cycles could apply to different cultures, countries, governments, businesses, organisations, and each individual's journey through their lives.

In this narrative, each stage of life could be divided into different stages with relevant strategies and work approaches to achieve those objectives. The life cycles, which I understood, consisted of the following stages-

1. Dream stage
2. Striving
3. Learning
4. Stagnation
5. New learning
6. Growth
7. Continuous learning and its application in real-life situations

For my graduate degree, I was admitted to Birla College, Pilani (now known as Birla Institute of Technology and Science). By and large, students who registered were prepared to rough it out for the next few years. Most of the food articles were brought from outside and served as - breakfast, lunch, tea, and dinner. If one needed a cup of tea or coffee, one had to make their own arrangements. Cold or hot weather did not matter. In summer, most of us brought a small table fan and kept water in earthen pitchers, which had some cooling impact on the water. Temperatures in summer could go up to 43-44 degrees Celsius and in winters could go down to 3-6 degrees Celsius.

So, once in Pilani, there were no distractions (no TVs, telephones, computers, movie halls, malls, restaurants, etc.) and the focus was only on studies. There was learning about coping with these challenges, like managing life on your own at the age of 16, tough coursework, and delivering projects in short time spans. It required commitment, hard work, perseverance (Chapter 14), and learning at a very fast pace within a timeline. Learning with focused attention and hard work brought me within the top three in the class of 1959.

Chapter-2

Striving Stage

'Learn as if you will live forever, live like you will die tomorrow.'

– Mahatma Gandhi

At BITS, most of the faculty had an overseas degree, were very committed to the teaching profession, and shared their knowledge freely. They were not only good teachers professionally but also good coaches. One of them used to invite a class on a Sunday for lunch and answer all questions we had in chemistry. We learnt in these free question-and-answer sessions (without inviting cynicism or meanness), and it was a great experiment in learning.

In the final years of the environment, we learnt to dream, and many of us felt like emulating one of those great professors who were our role models.

I felt that getting an overseas degree is a must for future growth. At that stage, I had no idea how that could be achieved. But a dream is a dream and unreal until realised.

The immediate objective was to be ahead of the competition and fulfil the dream of higher studies at one of the universities in the USA. At that stage, it was not clear which specialisation and which university.

Once out of Pilani, the goal was to find a job that would allow building adequate funds to meet preliminary expenses before starting higher studies. Also, the assumption was that there would be an assistantship available during the proposed studies period. There was no entrance tests required for a master's degree admission at that time, and it was purely based on the scorecard of the graduate degree.

The objective was to earn and save adequate money in the next 2-3 years to reach the UK or USA to pursue further education.

I was helped by an alumnus of BITS who helped me to connect with a Pharma unit called Jagson Pal Labs in Delhi, and I got my first job as an analytical chemist for INR 150 per month. The first assignment was challenging, with a lot of learning and a great experience. However, it turned out that life in Delhi was costly, and the opportunity to save and grow was negligible.

Within 3 months of my working, I had an offer of INR 200 per month at a nearby small town called Kanpur as a chemist, which later allowed me to upgrade my position as a manufacturing chemist. I was lucky that my sister, who lived in Kanpur, happily agreed to arrange for my stay. My plan was to save as much as possible in the next 2-3 years. The dream was getting more intense, but I struggled to find a way forward.

Since I was in Pilani on my own and had no mentor, all decisions had to be taken after a debate between the conscious mind and the 'Inner self' (Inner self can be described as your core values and some sense of identity and a feeling of who you are).

Self-awareness is about the ability to recognise that you are different and capacity to recognise your thoughts and feelings. 'Inner self' is especially crucial when important decisions have to be made, resulting in the best possible solution at that point in time.

I used to have 'Self-talk' whenever I was in a difficult situation regarding decision-making. This 'Inner Self' sometimes did not offer many options except to advise learning to persevere and continue to work hard, so as to realise the dream. This is also crucial to be self-disciplined so that our lives run as we want them to run in order to achieve our goals.

> **'It does not matter whether you are pursuing success in business or personal life in general, the bridge between wishing and accomplishing is discipline.'**
>
> **– Harvey Mackay**

A disciplined life is a structured life, focused on the goal backed by adequate efforts. Self-discipline provides confidence to make right decisions and in case of a rare failure, accepts the blame instead of assigning it to a person or something in the environment.

With my focused attention on my goal, I was looking for a better-paying job and a low-cost place to live. After a year, I found one higher-salaried job which helped me to reach my financial goal faster. There was no internet at that time; I had to find some names of the universities from the library of the US embassy that were offering student assistantship while pursuing a higher degree simultaneously.

I got my applications typed and posted by 'Air Mail'. I wrote to around ten universities and waited for replies, which used to take 5-6 weeks. It was a time for practising, patience, and perseverance.

Normally, regret letters came faster than those considered for admission. It was now Jan '61, and I was seeking admission for the term beginning in Sep '61. My 'inner self' feedback was that I would get admission and an assistantship in one of those ten institutions and should prepare for departure in early September '61.

Air India ticket to New York was about INR 3000, and the exchange rate was INR 5 to a US$. At that time, applying for a visa was a very lengthy process, and I had made enquiries about the time it takes and criteria for approval.

I had felt many times that there was an 'inner self' which was guiding each step of mine as there was nobody else who had experience of a similar journey, and I kept moving as per my plan with higher self-confidence.

First week of Feb 61 was the best week when I received three offers and had to decide which one to choose without having much knowledge of the projects running in those universities. The condition of admission offered was that I had to confirm my joining date within 4 weeks of receiving the offer letter.

All I could think of was getting some advice from one of my teachers who was a Ph.D. from the US and who addressed most of my queries. I had an offer from University of Buffalo (now called the State University of New York), and they had received a NIH grant, and a group of scientists from different universities had formed a strong Medicinal Chemistry group. This group was also looking for competent students and post-doctoral fellows.

The offer was from Professor David J. Koch, School of Pharmacy, University of Buffalo. Professor David's group of scientists was engaged in developing molecules that could work as anticancer compounds. It required a good background in synthetic organic chemistry, and we had good exposure at BITS, Pilani. I finally decided to join this group at SUNY at Buffalo, NY, in the USA.

I was delighted with the adequate savings of two years' work. I got my wardrobe and ticket made so that I could join in mid-September 1961.

The Government of India allowed about USD 200 to meet the expenses during the journey and until I received my first stipend of USD 200 for the month.

My flight on Air India with stopovers in Beirut and London took me to New York. I had a colleague in NY who guided me to the Greyhound bus point for travel to Buffalo, NY. I reached Buffalo around 7 pm and asked a porter to recommend a nearby hotel. He advised that there is a good place to stay just a block away, so I could walk there with my suitcase. I found the hotel and asked for a room for a few nights at $20 per night. The next morning, I got ready to go to the School of Pharmacy at the University of Buffalo by a bus journey of twenty-five minutes from the hotel in downtown.

On arrival at the School of Pharmacy, I was advised to go to the third floor where I found Dr. Davids's office.

As I knocked on the door, he came out and said that he was expecting me, gave me a warm welcome, and asked if I would like a cup of coffee. He walked down to the adjacent hall and brought two cups of coffee. He also suggested that I could take off my jacket and tie to be more comfortable. It was a warm and sunny day, and university sessions had not started yet.

In my discussion with Dr. David, I reemphasised that my family has agreed for two years to complete my master's and return home. Dr. David heard and gave no answer. I assumed that my request has been registered and I will follow the master's programme.

By the time my induction was over, it was lunchtime, and one of his students, John, asked me if I would like to go out for lunch with him. I was a vegetarian until I reached Buffalo.

For lunch, John, who was quick to develop friendships, drove for 20 minutes in his Beetle and stopped at a McDonald's restaurant. He enquired if I wished to have a burger or a cheeseburger. Spontaneously, I agreed to have a cheeseburger as it sounded more familiar than a regular burger. I was hungry, and the cheeseburger with French fries and coke turned out to be a good lunch.

One of my colleagues was fussy about food and used to cook lentils, rice, and vegetables every day, spending 2-3 hours on cooking. It resulted in him being behind in classwork, finally failing and having to return home. The adaptability and management of change are difficult for some. Such individuals do not address what the goal is and why they are there.

That was one thing, which I had decided that nothing was more important than completing my degree requirements in the shortest period of time.

Next day, the professor explained the coursework required for the degree. Dates for weekly or monthly examinations were not revealed; therefore, students had to be ready all the time. The process of teaching was very different from what I had experienced. For example, the Professor of Chemistry, in the first session, said, "Please get through the first five chapters of the chemistry book, and we will start from the sixth chapter in the next class."

He had covered all three boards fixed on all three sides of the walls of the lecture hall. There was a quiz every week for 10 minutes and was counted in the total score of the course. First examinations were conducted after 4-5 weeks of the course commencement, and I scored 60-70 points in each of them. In my coursework in India, above sixty points were regarded as an 'A' equivalent of the US system. When I got the papers back, I thought it is a fairly good performance, especially in view of my two years break in studies while I was doing jobs. When I met Professor David the next day, he appeared quite grim and asked if I had understood the implications of my scores in the various examinations. I replied that these are good from the education system I am coming from, to which his answer was, these all are close to "F" (fail) in all four courses in the first semester. The degree requires B plus as an average, and if I was unable to get this average score, I will not be permitted to continue the postgraduate course. This was my first failure, and I had no choice but to succeed.

2.1 CHALLENGES AND FACING THE BRUTE SQUARELY

There emerged two simultaneous priorities in my mind. Firstly, how to score 90+ in the next three examinations in all four subjects and secondly, to save enough funds ($300) in four months for a return ticket in case my efforts did not fructify.

I did not have any communication with my 'inner self' for a few weeks, and when facing this unusual situation, it was natural for me to contact and seek guidance and validate my way forward. I needed a lot of reassurance and motivation to move into a very challenging phase of the journey of my life. The answer came quickly-

'Put in your best, single-mindedly and you shall succeed. It's not beyond you.'

It was a big encouragement and reassurance to pursue the chosen path.

From then on, I was not thinking of any downsides that could possibly emerge and moved on as if I was possessed by an energy that had never been experienced before. There was no thought of a possible failure. I had never been shy of meeting challenges head-on, and this was the first one at Buffalo.

Also, saying I remembered was-

'Focus on what you can control, accept what you can't, and ultimate inner strength through wisdom and virtue.'

– Stoic

As the validated action plan emerged, I decided to move to cheaper accommodation the next day, which turned out to be in an attic and at half the rent I was paying earlier.

Next action was to focus on studies and invest as many hours as humanly possible. The library closed at midnight; therefore, studies had to shift to the attic. Coffee made from hot water from the tap helped my systems run in fifth gear. A 16-hour-a-day routine was just about enough to keep a little ahead of the coursework.

Everything else looked unimportant, and the coursework occupied the frontal cortex 24/7. As per our approved strategy, I was also gradually moving towards my financial goal of collecting $300.

I reached a stage when I could recall the salient points of each chapter and felt I could answer most of the questions. Revisions after revisions built a confidence, which was lacking after the first examination. Second and third months tests yielded B plus to A plus scores and I met the average above A for the semester.

After the results were out, one afternoon, my three faculty professors collectively invited me for coffee and congratulated me on maintaining the average grade of the semester for the postgraduate programme.

These professors shared their earlier apprehension that I might not be able to score and might have to return to India in Jan '63.

They were all happy that I had qualified to pursue my degree and said that I demonstrated commitment, quick learning, and achieving the objective well.

This was an example of converting a potential failure into success through sheer determination and hard work, resulting in a satisfactory outcome.

2.2 SEARCH FOR THE UNKNOWN BEGINS

The following week in Jan '63, a project was assigned to me which was to establish a possible role of biotin in carboxylation in the first step of the synthesis of lipid metabolism. It required the opening of the five-membered ring of biotin, the capability of its amino group to pick up a carboxyl group and possibly transfer it to Acetyl-CoA.

Research project work brought in learning of deeper internal scrutiny **"which encouraged not to give up and continue efforts with vigour relentlessly."**

The research project appeared close to impossible, and my mind wandered and at times slipped into self-doubt. The function of biotin was unknown, and there was a possibility it might not work, and one has to abandon the approach and sometimes the project. These unknowns created a fear of failure.

I was simultaneously exploring other pathways of opening the five-membered ring and developing options. The strategy was that if one pathway fails, have alternative routes ready, select the best option with a higher probability of success, and then conduct preliminary experimental trials.

This learning was known as **strategic thinking** and a path to go from point A to point B. Evaluate options so that one has an alternate route available. Install markers to monitor that one is on track and within the timelines agreed with your own self.

My 'inner self' was stronger than ever before and supporting me right through with messages like -

'Keep going, you shall succeed.'

The following eight-month project work led to a breakthrough when the biotin ring opened up and could react with carbon dioxide. This experiment was repeated six times, and then it was decided to send the first communication through a scientific publication. The task was to establish the robustness of the process and explore a few other alternatives.

In the following 18 months' time, the project and coursework were completed for a master's degree. It was time to check where I was after 18 months and where I was going. I, therefore, decided to meet Dr. David on a Friday afternoon.

> **'It is only when we take chances that our lives improve. The initial and the most difficult risk we need to take is to become honest.'**
>
> **– Walter Anderson**

2.3 CHANGE OF STRATEGY – LARGER PICTURE-VISION

I explained to Dr. David that my intent was to do a master's degree in 2 years and then move on to a job.

He heard me out and said, 'Listen, your project has gone very well and in fact beyond my expectations. If you could possibly continue another 18-24 months on the second part of this project, you could qualify for a Ph.D. So, think about it seriously and revert back to me by next Friday.'

I was taken aback, since I had not considered doing a Ph.D. I was confused for a day, but during the long weekend, I had enough time to get myself into knots and later needed to undo with the help of my 'inner self' system to guide me to reach a right conclusion. There was no way to contact my parents, but I was aware that they would be disappointed by my extension of stay, by two more years. I also did not have a colleague or mentor who could participate in the decision-making process.

I had to weigh up all pros and cons since the offer of doing a Ph.D. in the following two years was very attractive. One of the reasons for this offer was that Dr. David had grants for projects from NIH and required experienced hands to complete some of those projects.

I had become accustomed to a 16-hour-a-day routine - 12 hours for project work and the remaining 4 hours for my coursework. I was confident that I would be able to meet my revised **goal** on time if I wanted to pursue my Ph.D. work.

Dr. David was away on his lecture tour for a few days, so I got to see him on the following Friday. The first clarification I sought was what all will be required, and what if it gets delayed.

He was reassuring and said:

'You have already completed more than half of the coursework, your project is halfway done, so I do not see any roadblocks in meeting your timeline'.

I was happy with his statement and agreed to continue for my Ph.D. requirements.

2.4   NEW ROLE AND NEW APPROACH

Life continued with new energy and led me to a faster pace. Project work yielded desired results. We had reported our findings in the 'Journal of Pharmaceutical Sciences' every six months resulting in three publications. We could prove in vitro studies that biotin indeed is capable of transferring CO_2 group and possibly participates in the first step of protein synthesis. The biotin project was completed within 18 months from the time I had agreed to pursue Ph.D. studies.

Once again there was a need to review where we are now and where we wished to go in the next twelve to sixteen months. Since I had a single purpose in my mind, I was very focused and was monitoring my progress every weekend. In a discussion, when I enquired what next, the answer was 'that a Ph.D. is not awarded in less than 3 years' time and you will be given another project which will add to your experience. However, that will not be included in your Ph.D. dissertation. I was dumbfounded and wondered how one can be so self-centred. My 'inner self' advised me to go along with the proposal and continue my focus on the project.

Within the following five months, 14-16 hours a day, I was able to generate certain leads which indicated that it could be a good project for a new student who joins for a Ph.D. degree.

I very frankly asked Dr. David why I was not being asked to appear for the final Ph.D. examination. I was counselled that now you have developed adequate skills and ready to take examination.

Furthermore, he said that you can wrap up the project work now and return for your final examination after a month's time.

The date was 20 March '65. I was pleased with the outcome but wondered if this was a ploy to flunk me and then give me the next examination after six months (that was the rule prevailing at that time).

I wound up my project work in seven days and decided to devote a full 16 hours a day to revise all I have covered in all the courses in the last 3 years. In the examination, any question could be asked that was covered during my stay of more than three years.

I was totally lost as to where to start. There was nobody who could guide or advise. The solution came from within – 'go through the whole lot and do your best.'

I had my mattress on the floor, had adequate food to last a week, and notes and books scattered all around.

I started from a zero base and completed the total coursework in 25 days. There was no sleeping time or routine; it was a continuous roll and only focused on learning. There were many situations where I had to do some work in the library to understand some of the concepts. I revised the following two days and was struggling to hold onto all that learning and was very uncomfortable. It was a Friday, and I decided, "that is enough and no more." I took a trip to downtown, saw a film, had dinner at my favourite restaurant, and came back. The next day, Sunday, I was totally blank in my thought process and peaceful.

Monday morning, I went to Dr. David's office.

He asked me to sit down in his office with white sheets of paper, pencils, and an eraser on the table. There, on the blackboard was a question written about suggesting the most appropriate route to the synthesis of an anticancer compound. It required knowledge of different aspects of synthetic chemistry, and one had to describe the right steps which were scientifically proven.

I started recalling all the steps and attempting to build the most appropriate route of synthesis. It was not from whatever we had done in coursework; rather, it was a research project being pursued in some other laboratory on the West coast. It was obvious to me that there was no correct answer, but I was aware that my approach had to be theoretically correct. Initially, it took me some time to grasp the situation, and suddenly the whole concept of synthesis emerged. It took me about 3 hours to design a synthetic route, and I revised it once again for any slip-ups. After the review, I was ready to submit my answer paper.

Dr. David asked if I would like to revise, and my answer was "not anymore." Whatever could be done has been done.

He said, "You come back at 4 pm, and we will let you know if you have cleared the examination or not." I was blank in my mind and was in a state where 'nothing mattered'.

I went out, had my lunch, and slept for an hour. Got ready to hear the final verdict on my month-long revision. I had purged all negative thoughts and was prepared to accept the result, whichever way it went. This was most probably based on my understanding that I had prepared well and was satisfied with my effort.

At 4 pm sharp, I knocked on the door of his office and found three of my senior faculty members who all together said, "Congratulations, Dr. Bhargava." I was choked with emotions, and it was hard to utter, "Thank you all." They asked me to take a seat at the conference table, offered me coffee and a doughnut, and complimented me on my outstanding coursework and the way the project was completed. After a few minutes, I came out in the lab, and all my colleagues congratulated me and invited me to a get-together in the evening to celebrate my newly acquired title.

2.5   CHOICE OF ROLE OF THE FUTURE

On the following Monday, Dr. David asked me if I would join him as a post-doctoral fellow, and I reminded him that I am keen to join an industrial group. I was aware that without his recommendation, getting a job in the us would be difficult. Since I did not have a job in the US, he felt I could be persuaded. I was given an additional project after the completion of my Ph.D. project, which I had accepted until I got an appointment in some industrial unit.

My confidence was based on the upcoming meetings with the two British international units, Imperial Chemical Industries and Unilever from the UK, who were visiting the campus to recruit fresh British-origin graduates as part of the reversal of the "Brain Drain" programme. I had registered with the Placement Centre of the university for these meetings.

I met the ICI plc Research Director and HR Director, and the interview lasted about 3 hours. There was nothing about my academic performance, but the discussion was a comparison of the British vs. American education system. Luckily, I had not only studied hard but also attempted to understand American culture and connected activities.

I had the advantage of learning from the detailed discussions with a group of British students who were working with another professor on the same floor. My response on comparison was quite accurate, and the interviewers were pleased to see a fresh Ph.D., explaining the systems with confidence.

At the end of that meeting, I was given a list of thirty vacancies and was asked to select three positions which will suit my background the best. I was also informed that I will receive a message within 7-10 days, and I will have to confirm acceptance immediately after.

Simultaneously, Unilever was looking for candidates for their R&D at Sunport, UK. They had changed the venue for my meeting from the campus to New York on a Saturday.

I appeared for the meeting at 11 am at the place of the HR Director who was watching American football and asked me, 'Param, I do not understand this game, can you please explain to me.' Since I was interested in this game and was a fan of the 'Buffalo Bills', I explained most of the details on the TV screen. I was always keen to learn about education systems, cultures, sports, etc. It is important to be aware of the environment beside pursuing the primary goal.

At 12:30, he said, "Can you join us for lunch where the Technical Director will also participate?" At 1 pm, we met in the restaurant, and after preliminary pleasantries, he asked about my Ph. D. project. I explained for about forty five minutes, and the discussion turned to what their needs were and where I fit in. I screened through their list of thirty-five jobs and indicated in which three jobs I would have the best fit.

I was also told that I will get a message within 7–10 days and if selected all transfer expenses will be borne by Unilever. I was confident that meetings had gone well, and I would receive appointments from both units.

There was another development where a Pharma unit in New Jersey wanted a Ph. D. in Chemistry and took me around their facility and wanted me to join as a permanent employee.

The only condition was that I would need to apply for a Green Card, and I should be looking for a long-term engagement. At that stage, I was unwilling to commit to any long-term assignment, and therefore, I had to politely decline the offer.

All this happened in the first 15 days of March 1965. I was keen to join one of the units that did not need Dr. David's recommendation. I wanted to finish the project and move on to my next role. Here again, I knew about ICI in India but was not very aware of Unilever's presence. Also, I always had at the back of my mind that I must have an option in case I needed to return to India for family reasons. I, therefore, accepted ICI plc's offer and informed them that I would join on 1st July 1965 after a 3-month break in India.

With all that happening, I went to Dr. David and informed him that I have appointments in the UK and would like to be released as soon as possible. He wondered how I got those jobs without his recommendations!

Finally, he agreed that if I can finish my project work in a week's time and hand it over to a colleague of mine in the laboratory, I will be allowed to leave. At the end of March, I made a reservation for my return ticket for early April.

My parents were pleasantly surprised when I reached their place and were delighted. Little did they know that in three months' time I would be joining ICIplc in the UK. They wanted me to take up a job in India, so I decided to explore three Government Institutes where I presented my Ph. D. work. All three appreciated my work and were willing to offer me a job. However, the facilities were inadequate, and seniority was the criterion for growth, which did not meet my needs.

In between, I found my life partner, and we went back in June '65 to join Imperial Chemical Industries, R&D unit at Blackley Site in Manchester in the UK.

Chapter-3

Learning Stage

> **'Success is the sum of the small efforts repeated day in and day out.'**
>
> **– Robert Collier**

Learning at Imperial Chemical Industries in Blackley, Manchester, UK.

On 1 July 65, my immediate superior, Section Leader Dr. Neil Dorby, welcomed me. He explained the organisation, different scientist doing different projects. introduced me to the other six scientists in his group, each of whom was aged 50+ and were engaged in finding new molecules in the dyestuffs and pigments field. At that time, ICI plc was one of the leaders in that segment worldwide. I was assigned a workbench and provided with a young chemist. I was given a project in which four methyl groups of durene were to be oxidised to serve as a nucleus for several dyestuffs.

I went around and looked at the facilities and realised that it will need quite a bit of upgradation to match the US facilities.

R&D Director called me after seven days, asked me how I was doing and how I found the facilities. I was quite open and frank with him, and I said I am fine, and people are quite happy with their routine, and each one devotes 4-6 hours to work. He sensed that I was not coming out with the full story and enquired what changes we should make to upgrade our facility. I said frankly, you need to start with a cultural change. Analytical Instruments, Library facilities are not up to international level. Scientists are orthodox in their approach, and R&D is not goal-directed. I could see he was a little uncomfortable listening to my comments and said 'Listen Param, I am aware of much information you presented, but the purpose to get you here is to bring that change, and I want you to write me a paper on all changes you envision except the culture and behaviour part, and present it to the R&D Board in a week from now.'

After my dealings with Dr. Davis, I had learnt that if you are thinking first about organisation and later your personal growth, there are very few roadblocks you are likely to have. That allowed me to be constructive, have the courage to share my views, and an attitude that solutions could be found even for insoluble problems. I was gradually turning less fearful and was not afraid of expressing my views amongst seniors.

Following week, the presentation was well received, and a team of three was formed to evaluate the needs in order of priority. I was also asked to participate in the project work sponsored by ICI plc in various universities. Initially, the R&D Director and I visited three universities to propose or follow projects. I had developed a good working relationship, and we were determined to upgrade the facility and later shift to a competitive, result-oriented culture. The journey indicated all signs of a successful time ahead. However, my Section Leader was not quite happy with the developments and called me the following day to review the progress of the project. I was given a project in which durene's methyl groups needed to be converted to four carboxylic groups. These were strong templates for various types of dyes and pigments. Later, I came to know that a local scientist, Dr. Brown, had worked for two years without successful conversion.

As the project was a difficult one, I was looking for unconventional ways to oxidise with an appropriate catalyst. The first 20 days brought no results, and working 12-14 hours a day was of no avail.

Being optimistic, I knew that sooner rather than later it would happen. I had developed a habit in the US to be in the library for about 2 hours each day to learn new developments and get a fresh outlook of the present. Here at ICI plc, I followed that practice, which I thought was a good practice. I had planned to be in the library for 1-2 hours, and Neil had seen me there on a few occasions. In the weekly review of the project, he advised me to spend more time on the project instead of in the library.

Luckily, two days before this meeting, I had come across a Czech journal with an English summary of a process that could be applicable to my project. I patiently listened and said that I would certainly spend more time on the project. In fact, I used to stay late in the evenings until my reaction was complete, of which he was not aware. I designed a reaction using the process outlined in the Czech journal. It was a high-temperature, high-pressure reaction, so it had to be done in an appropriate reactor.

At 7 pm, I went to the basement where all these equipment were and requested the In-charge of that Section to allow an autoclave for carrying out the reaction.

It was designed for 18 hours, so the next day at noon, I got the contents of the autoclave and brought them to my lab to test if conversion had taken place or not. While I was doing that test, the Research Director dropped in to check how things were and also asked what the material was that I was working on. I explained to him all I had done and indicated that possibly we have achieved the conversion.

He asked me to come to his office and also called my Section Leader and said,

"Neil, do you know Param has most probably achieved the breakthrough that Dr Brown had been attempting for the last few years and had left for academia?"

He also ordered some tea and Gingernut biscuits. This is how he appreciated my work and said - if your findings confirm that you have got, I will like you to present this in the next R&D Executive review meeting. I observed Neil kept quiet during this transaction. The next day, Neil called and asked how come he was not informed, and the Director knew about it. I apologised and briefed him about the event, but apparently, he was not convinced. I completed the project in the following months and got on to the next project.

Learning, focused attention, and the 'will to succeed' were the key elements to materialise the goal.

The R&D Director was committed to upgrading the labs and culture of the place. I was asked to write a paper on what was required to bring it up to a level matching the US facilities. Most of the staff had not used modern equipment, and a five-day exposure at a university was arranged for newly hired chemists. By that time, I had developed a sound working relationship with my Director. We explored how we could work with different universities by sponsoring some projects which had potential but were important from a long-term point of view.

By December '66, we had made considerable progress, and I was informed that if I continued to perform well, I could be the youngest-ever Section Leader in few years' time.

Unfortunately, winters were harsh on us as coal was being used during winter days to keep residences warm.

The pollution was very high. When I met my GP, he advised me that if we wanted to stay well, we should consider returning to the 'sunshine country' - India. A large population in this area suffers from respiratory illnesses.

Since we were experiencing breathing difficulties, I shared with my R&D Director who reluctantly agreed and said, "I will get you placed in one of the ICI India's R&D sections." True to his word, he made contact with the Indian subsidiary and found there was an opening in Calcutta. However, he said the compensation package is too low and I need a week to finalise this transfer on reasonable terms.

He certainly was quick, and his counterparts in India responded as some of them knew him before their secondment to India. Finally, I was offered a position and was allowed to return around Christmas time, '66.

Chapter-4

The Challenge

> **'Our ability to handle life's challenges
> is a measure of our strength of character.'**
>
> **– Les Brown**

I landed in Calcutta on 2nd Jan 67 and was introduced to my superiors and colleagues. Initially, a one-month training was at Tiljala laboratory, Calcutta, but there were plans to move the laboratory and Technical Service function to the Works site at Rishra, about twenty-five km from Calcutta.

ICI India's head office was located in Calcutta, and Rishra was the first site in India where ICI India had set up their manufacturing facilities in 1939. The manufacturing facilities included Alkali and chemicals, Rubber Chemicals, Paints, and Polythene. It was a large site of about 75 acres, and most of the staff were housed in the nearby ICI-owned housing complex. The Managing Director, Robert Railey, a Scotsman, was also housed in the same complex.

All plants had managers who were brilliant chemical engineers and were very capable. Rishra had an abundance of talented minds. The side effect was that there was a very high level of competition, and evenings were more about identifying issues and establishing to whose proposal was less complex to actualise.

I was placed in the R&D of Rubber Chemicals Business, which was not fully established. Within a year, I was transferred to the chemicals production unit to learn technology and manpower management. The facility was manned well by several competent chemical engineers. I, being an outsider, was not accepted immediately and was given a project that involved a hazardous chemical to handle. I walked through, and after a six-month training period, I was given the responsibility to manage it.

As an R&D chemist, I had no idea of manufacturing plants, especially those that are hazardous, operating at high temperatures and high pressures.

Operators were highly trained, but one mistake and there would be a major accident or disaster. Reactors were on the first floor, and liquids were pumped from underground storage tanks to measuring vessels installed at a height of twelve feet above the reactor. The liquids were added by gravity, the vessel closed, and heated to stipulated temperatures, which also generated high pressures. We were at a stage when we were running at full capacity and were considering expansion. My creative self-got into action and decided to plan a series of experiments to determine when the reaction was actually complete. These processes were based on 1962 technology, and whatever time it might have taken at that time was decided as the batch cycle time - 72 hours.

We planned to take samples every eight hours and found that the reaction was complete in 36 hours. Exhaustive technological evaluations were done, and the product was found comparable to the one made in 72 hours. Thus, we had doubled capacity, and major investment was not required.

Second major learning was to keep a team of 150 individuals motivated so that productivity levels improved significantly.

This was done through communications on the shop floor, and the ability to empathise with the workforce. There were more successes and fewer failures.

In these times, labour was restive and aggressive, and with the communist Government in West Bengal, we had new demands every month. On very small issues, there would be strikes, *dharnas* or the "block passage of entry and exit" of the plant. We were trained to run continuous plants on very short notice.

The work had become routine except for manpower issues of varying intensities arising every week. This challenge occupied the minds of most of the managers. In that environment, one could do very little except keep operations safe.

The time had come when I felt there was no new learning, and spending time in repetitive activity was a bad investment of time. I wondered what possible options were open since opportunities in those times outside were fewer, and not many considered moving from a company like ICI India. I had a choice to 'take it easy' as some advised or be proactive about a change.

STAGNATION

Use of Influencing Skills

A new MD had come in 1976, and he used to invite staff on Friday evenings for a get-together and was feeling his way to how Rishra's (an industrial township 25 km from Calcutta) culture is and how it operates. In one of those evenings, I shared my background and longer stay in the plant and also concerns about inadequacies of the business - like gaps in the product range and competition gaining market share. We needed to develop our own R & D strategy so that these 4-5 products can be offered to our customers in next few years and thus an immediate need to expand R&D. The MD promised to revert back the following week.

I was aware there were major product gaps in the Rubber Chemicals portfolio compared to international players. ICI plc had exited from this business in the early 70s in the UK, so support from the parent company was not available. Our R&D was too small to cater to such major projects.

ICI India's concern was that the business was doing reasonably well, but long-term survival depended on bridging the gaps in the product portfolio. Our competitors in India were Monsanto and Bayer.

There were four major gaps in the product mix of the business.

1. PEPTISER

Bayer had this product in their range and was importing it from their mother plant in WG. The intermediate required was not available in India. We developed the process and after exhaustive testing, scaled up in the pilot plant and sourced out intermediate manufacturing. The final step of its conversion to the final product was undertaken in our plant successfully.

Initially, there were some technical issues that were investigated and rectified. The modified product was well received by the customers since it was locally made, and customers wanted to have a local source of supplies instead of depending on a single imported source.

2. RETARDER

Second gap in the product range was a safer retarder, which was also being imported by Monsanto for India. It was a complex synthesis, and this project development work was jointly done with our Central Research and Development set up in Mumbai which had a large group of very learned scientists. The synthesis was pursued jointly by Central R&D group and Rishra labs. It was a difficult project as by-product formation was high and thus active materials yields were low.; It took us a year to establish a suitable process.

Once the process was ready, we undertook trials at our pilot plant and conducted minor modifications so that it could be adopted on a plant scale. Central Research and Development was deeply involved in it, and the improved process gave acceptable yields, etc. There were issues around purity and yield, and these were studied and took about 6 months' time to overcome these inefficiencies.

After exhaustive performance trials it was launched in the market and major customers were happy to have a reliable local source of supply vs, the imported by our competitor.

3. ANTIOXIDANT

There was a need for a low-cost antioxidant, especially in small and medium industries. It was a complex mix of several polymers of aniline. This product was manufactured in India by Bayer.

Our labs were engaged for about two years before we could conduct a pilot plant trial. Once a product matching that of Bayer was established, it had to be evaluated by the Technical Service team and then at customers' premises.

Once the repeatability of pilot trials was well established, a proposal was prepared for manufacturing at plant scale.

It needed a glass-lined vessel because of the corrosive nature of the catalyst. We happened to have one as a spare in stock, and the plant was designed and installed in the following six months.

Initial plant trials did not yield the right quality of product.

We had to go back to the lab to identify the reason for this variance, and the catalyst dosage had to be adjusted.

The batches after this correction met the specifications and were sent for evaluation to the technical laboratory and two customers.

Initially, two complaints of lump formation were received, and after that, the process got stabilised, and commercial production started. It was a successful introduction to the range, and slowly we were getting closer to our rightful market share.

On a personal side in 1981, I was appointed as an Application Research and Development Manager for Rubber Chemicals. This meant additional responsibility for Technical Service, which required extensive travelling.

4. ANTIOZONANT-ZC

While we were bridging the gaps in the product range, the major gap was this Antiozonant that Bayer and Monsanto had in their range in India.

During this period, we had put the Antiozonant project on the back burner as we had encountered roadblocks and felt helpless to progress any further.

Neither did we have a process nor a plan to develop those complex steps of synthesis with local knowledge and the facility in the pilot plant. The issue was that seniors had a different perception. Some thought it was simple and could be developed in our own labs, while some felt that the process could be developed but the technology to manufacture at 3000 tonnes per annum was difficult.

A few weeks later, the newly appointed MD focused on business needs and found that we are stuck on this project. In a discussion, it was decided that we should find a solution either by developing a local process or finding a suitable supplier of the technology. The MD was convinced that this product was critical for the long-term survival of the business.

I was aware of some of the exploratory work done earlier; therefore, it was easier to establish the needs for this project. One of the major requirements was a high-pressure and high-temperature autoclave.

(For a two-step conversion of the intermediate to the final product.) These autoclaves were available in Europe and the USA, and the delivery time was 9-12 months besides the higher prices. I decided to go and see different labs that were using similar autoclaves in the northern part of India. During my visit, I came across an autoclave at one of the National Laboratories, which was from WG with a delivery period of 9 months. I found the name of the agent in India who happened to be in Delhi. A nine-month delivery period was a big discouragement, but I had made up my mind to meet this agent and at least understand the process.

Next day at 11 am, I was the first customer in his workshop. He was polite and intrigued by my urgency as he was aware that most of the projects take years. I explained to him about my new assignment, and the project depended on the availability of a high-temperature, high-pressure autoclave. Since he was dealing with this kind of equipment and appreciated my urgency, he asked for a few hours to check the status of autoclaves on order and at sea. I went away, and after two hours, I returned. He informed me that there is one at sea likely to dock at Mumbai port in the next 10 days and agreed to divert this autoclave meeting our specifications to us. However, he put a condition that I needed to make full payment by evening to reserve this autoclave for us.

I requested to allow me 24 hours, but he was adamant, and I left saying that I will come back by 5 pm. I reached the Delhi office and communicated with the MD, and he, in return, got the Delhi Manager authorised to arrange the payment. I did go back at 3 pm to him and handed over the payment. I requested that I have "Delivered my promise", and he needs to honour his side of the commitment. He smiled and said that the ship has docked, and you will receive it in Calcutta in a week's time.

I was delighted and informed the MD the same evening. I was aware that engineering systems were highly process-oriented and would prioritise my installation work as per their processes and provide me a slot as per their list of pending jobs. I, therefore, got two of the engineers attached to R&D and shared my concern. They both were excited to participate in my project and said it can be done independently of the central system if done outside office hours. I assured nothing untoward would be allowed to happen and prepared for installation so that it could be done within 24 hours of its arrival at our Works.

It so happened that the autoclave arrived within 5 days, and we received it in the afternoon and waited until 4:30 pm when the plant hours were over. I had briefed the engineering team about the urgency of its installation.

There was a lot of enthusiasm and commitment from the whole team, so we started unpacking immediately after its arrival and began the task of installation. As per the plan, it was completed by the midnight, and we arranged for a water trial during the night shift.

The next morning, to our pleasant surprise, the autoclave held the pressure and temperatures to the specifications.

We got ready to carry out the first experiment of reducing a nitro function to an amino function of an intermediate of the final product.

The cycle was twelve hours, and intermittent testing was being done to test for the completion of the reaction. Luckily, it was completed in 8 hours, and I informed the MD who in turn communicated to the Chairman about this. He also congratulated the Works Manager for this breakthrough. Once the Works Manager knew, the first thing in the morning he visited the site with his engineer. He asked me all that I had done and cautioned me not to follow this procedure as it is against the standard operating procedures of the engineering Department. I agreed and reassured that this will not be repeated.

While leaving, the Works Manager said, "Well done, thanks." They both congratulated me for utilising my entrepreneurial spirit, energy, and speed, which was hitherto unknown in the system-oriented organisation.

After this limited success, I realised the difference between Science and Technology. This process, even if perfected at pilot scale, it would not have been possible to scale up to a 3000-tonne plant.

Therefore, the next step was to convince the decision-makers that this is not the way forward and we need to find a suitable technology partner.

Monsanto and Bayer were the world leaders and also our competitors in India.

I was asked, simultaneously, to search for a suitable technology partner. Once I got the approval, I sought an appointment with Uniroyal, Goodyear, and Goodrich in the USA. Uniroyal had the technology but was still working to improve the conversion efficiency so that it could be unprofitable in a competitive environment. They were reluctant to share any information. Since the technology was undergoing optimisation, Uniroyal could be an option in a few years. Goodyear and Goodrich were no longer manufacturing in this area, so no viable technology supplier was available from the US.

Sumitomo and Ouchi Shinko chemical industries were the other two in Japan.

Sumitomo had a 12,000-tonnes-per-annum plant running in Okayama.

Since our need was for a 3000-tonne per annum plant, Sumitomo was reluctant to work on downsizing the plant for us.

Our search of a few months did not yield any results and was a big disappointment.

While we were considering other possibilities, I was asked to present the progress of my three projects (Antiozonants, Engineering Plastics, Electrodes technology) which I was pursuing simultaneously, to ICI plc, UK, Board Director, responsible for India.

After the presentation, ICI plc's Board Director said-

"Param, if you have a hole in the roof of your house, you wanted to get a new car and your wife wanted to go on holidays, which one will you attend to first?" I said, obviously, "the hole in the roof." He continued and said, "Tell me which of these three projects is most urgent from a business needs point of view."

I immediately said "antiozonants." He further inquired what is blocking us from progressing. I narrated the whole story about my unsuccessful search for a technology partner.

Also, it was added that only Sumitomo had a running plant and technology but was reluctant to meet our requirement of a downsized plant. He asked me to provide him with details of the contacts and the dates I met Sumitomo in Osaka

It was a Friday, and that evening he was leaving and shared that he would contact Sumitomo on Monday and let us know the outcome the following week, on Monday or Tuesday.

True to his word, on Monday evening we received a message that an engineer and I should go to meet the In-charge of operations in Osaka, and they will explore the possibility of helping us out.

DETERMINATION TO SUCCEED

Within 10 days, we got ourselves organised and were on our way to Osaka. On arrival, we received a very warm reception.

The next day morning, we left for Okayama where their manufacturing facility was located. The first 2 days were spent explaining the details of our needs. The following three days involved discussions, including a plant visit, to identify the hurdles Sumitomo was likely to face in downsizing the plant from 12000 tonnes per annum to 3000 tonnes per annum.

Possible solutions were discussed and narrowed down to the two best options. We returned to India, briefed our seniors, and sought direction.

The Chairman and Overseas Director were informed by the MD and thanked the Overseas Director "for making something impossible, possible" for this business.

A business team was appointed to first negotiate the financial terms for the transfer of technology and once agreed, to identify competent engineers for designing and construction work, in close collaboration with the Japanese team. Our Works Engineer was a dynamic, knowledgeable, hardworking person with very high integrity. His support was of immense help in the projects we undertook during that period.

The existing plant had enough land area to accommodate the new plant, so no search for land, power, and water was required. Skilled manpower was sourced from the existing facility.

The ICI plc Board had asked how long it would take to complete the construction of the plant. After detailed discussions, we agreed on 18 months' time from the day the complete design work was handed over to the engineering team.

The whole business team was excited and highly motivated to complete the construction in 18 months, knowing very well all the hurdles likely to be faced, especially from equipment suppliers for high-temperature, high-pressure duty reactors.

Sumitomo team worked very hard to reduce the time taken to get detailed drawings and were on-site for 3 weeks to get us organised. We had engaged world-class engineering consultants, and they merged well with our team and gained momentum very quickly. There was a micro-planning template used to monitor each day's progress.

Each member of the team excelled at their targets and was tackling challenges that were beyond what they had experienced earlier. There was a 'can do' attitude across the team, and the project work was ahead of its target schedule.

Trial runs were conducted, and several issues cropped up on conversion efficiency and quality. The finished form was free-flowing granules, and this flow was dependent on the purity of the product.

Though impurity did not impact the performance, free flow was essential during handling for processing in rubber units.

These issues were resolved with the guidance of the Japanese team successfully. Our operations team also received training and was able to operate the plant without any outside help.

Since it was a major investment in West Bengal after a long time, the Chief Minister was approached for a formal inauguration, and he kindly agreed.

Preparations were made for his arrival, and inauguration by the Chief Minister of WB, Shri Jyoti Basu. It was a major investment in 1986 in that belt of WB and was regarded as a major achievement for the State Government of West Bengal as well as ICI India Ltd.

Sometime in July, after exhaustive trials, Accinox ZC - Antiozonant was launched specially for our customers looking for a reliable alternative source. The physical form was different from the competition and offered handling and mixing advantages.

On the successful launch of ZC and other products, I was informed that I have been appointed as the General Manager of Chemicals, and the following year as GM of Rubber Chemicals and Plastics responsible for P&L of these businesses.

Our major customers were happy that now ICI India could offer a full range, and they did not need to depend on our competitors.

Chapter-5

New Learning

MANAGEMENT OF CHANGE – PAINTS BUSINESS

> **'The success in life isn't based on your ability to simply change. It is based on your ability to change faster than your competition, customers and businesses.'**
>
> **– Mark Sanborn**

I was appointed GM-Commercial, Plastic and Chemicals in Oct '89. I learnt the fundamentals of sales and purchase and in Jul '90 was appointed as General Manager, Commercial.

While Rubber Chemicals was doing fairly well, my colleague who was running a larger business - Paints fell ill and had to return to Canada immediately. Since it was an international appointment, it could take up to 3 months to fill the vacancy.

I was asked on a Friday (Nov '92) to fill in as an interim GM Paints in addition to my existing business - Rubber Chemicals.

I was aware that the Paints business was not doing well, and we were number 3 or 4 in terms of market share. I also worked out that no miracles can happen in three months, and I will be able to hand over to a new leader 'as is where is' basis.

Since I had no exposure to the Paints business, I had an apprehension if, for some unknown reason, the business got worse, what would be the impact on the organisation and my own future. I conducted a risk analysis on the following basis-

I looked at the first six months of performance of the current year and compared it with two-quarters of earlier years. It was apparent that under the leadership of earlier GMs, the status had not improved. We had a group of leaders who had been running the business for some years. They were quite clear that this is the best one can do under the circumstances. There were genuine constraints, and the leadership was not able to find solutions. Sales could not be increased because we had a lesser number of salesmen and dealers. If sales were higher during seasonal months, plants were not able to deliver. Plants could not deliver because of unreliable suppliers. Thus, it was a vicious cycle and was difficult to know where to start.

Initially, I was also sympathetic, and then I realised that if nothing was done, the status quo would prevail. In unknown situations like this, I had always wanted to know the strengths and weaknesses of the team, why they do what they do, and what possible pathways for course corrections were available.

In the meantime, the newly appointed MD, Asia Pacific, decided to visit us for three days. I was asked to go and receive him at the airport. Our car journey to our guest house was about an hour, and we were discussing the environment, etc., and finally about the business.

Next day after the presentation of our strategy and a visit to the old Rishra plant, he appeared to be quite pleased.

There was an evening meeting with MD India, MD Asia Pacific, and two Board members. I was also invited. Post-dinner, a discussion took place, and MD Asia Pacific (AP) said Param is suitable for the job we have in Paints India. However, we will want him to operate full-time with in a year and disengage from the chemicals business. After some thought, MD India agreed and thus appointment was finalised.

Next day, I asked MD AP that I have no exposure to the Paints business, so how do you expect me to perform? MD AP's answer was that you will be alright. Next week, we have an international meet of top managers in Singapore, and you will join. After that, spend a week at the Brisbane plant, a week at the Sydney plant, and a week in Melbourne with me. By that time, you will know all you need to know. In return, all I will expect is a fifteen-minute review every Friday. MD AP encouraged me and reinforced my confidence. I also got his agreement to redesign the organisational structure in the following 3-4 months.

This is an example of curiosity, learning, hard work, and expressing your confidence to face new challenges.

On my return from Melbourne, with greater confidence, I began to reexamine the initial findings of the strategy and develop a modified action plan.

I had a learning mindset and delved into most aspects of the business. I had a fuzzy picture of what was not right, but careful analysis yielded the following outcome-

1. Supplies to customers were not on time and incomplete product mix.
2. Product gaps which were a handicap in the marketplace.
3. Our dealer network was one-third of the market leader.
4. Salesmen were one-fourth of the market leader, and we had an ageing team whose productivity was low.
5. Top leadership with a growth mindset was needed.

We had two manufacturing sites - one in Rishra and the other one in Hyderabad. We had a lower market share in the North-West and were strong in the East.

If the goal was to achieve rapid growth, which was 18-20%, we needed manufacturing facilities in the West, South, and North.

For the interim, we worked out a four-fold strategy for following three years-

1. Improve the supply chain so that OTIF (On Time and In Full) can be enhanced to increase customer satisfaction.
2. Increase the number of dealers (5000 to 10000) by offering high quality, timely delivery, and volume incentives in line with industry practice.
3. Also double the number of salesmen - "feet on the streets" to service most of the customers well and cover a wider area.
4. Induct dynamic, leaders with a growth mindset willing to bring about a major change in the way we operated. Talented internal and some external candidates were appointed to the Business.
5. Bridge the product gaps as soon as possible. We were aware that a new product launch can take 3-4 years after exhaustive trials.

We had a small product development laboratory in Hyderabad. To bridge the main gaps in the product range, market research with our own data and competitors' positioning was evaluated.

Several options were identified, and another round of re-examination yielded five products for development in the lab.

These five products were given to five different teams in the Research and Development group so that they are ready for market trials in 3-4 years' time simultaneously. Two of these products were already being pursued in the laboratory for two years, and it was important to demonstrate to get them in the market as quickly as possible. New scientists from a similar field were hired, testing and analytical instruments were added, and wherever possible space was added to the existing laboratory. Every two weeks, a review meeting was held to identify bottlenecks, if any, and assist in removing them.

Earlier, two products (exterior paint and another one in the lower segment) were about to be completed, and work was initiated to make them ready for market launch.

The first lower segment product was launched in Calcutta, and regional dealers were invited. The product was well received, and bookings exceeded our expectations.

The next issue was capacity, as the present orders could only be delivered in three months' time (based on the existing output).

Brainstorming resulted in support of increasing existing productivity by 25% and rewarding the workforce adequately.

Also, 33% more production resulted from supplementing the third shift manned by quality workers and a good management team. It was thus possible to start delivering orders in 6-8 weeks' time. The product was well received, and top-line growth could be seen after bridging those gaps.

We could experience Dulux brand revival and expansion with more and more dealers. This led to the building up of market confidence and was the start of the turnaround of ICI India's Paints business and its market share. The details are described in the following Chapter 6.

Growth Phase

'Life is growth. If we stop growing, technically and spiritually, we are as good as dead.'

– Morihei Ueshiba

Out of the five strategic priorities as per the 80/20 principle, Supply Chain improvement was the most crucial for the business. New experts were inducted, and the help of IT was sought. The right inventory, accurate production planning as per customer demand was done on the 25th of each month for the following month. No extra production was permitted even though plant capacities were available. Monitoring systems were put in place to ensure that supplies were reaching customers on time and in full. For the seasonal peak sales from August to November of the year, stocks had to be built up. Thus, four warehouses in four regions were reorganised to cope with higher supplies and higher sales.

Quality was the main focus, and each member was trained about the impact of quality on the product and service.

Credit to dealers was around 80-90 days. Business was often borrowing due to insufficient cash flow. Managing working capital was a significant challenge. During those times, one could borrow money at interest rates of 12-15%. We had substantial borrowings because customers were paying in 90 days and suppliers wanted advance or 30 days credit.

We had several rounds of discussions about the reduction of credit days for customers with our sales team, and the general view was that if the reduction of the credit limit was implemented, we would lose up to 15% of sales that year. It was a tough choice.

I was of the view that August is the time for correction, as dealers start stocking for the festival sales. The fear of loss of sales and thus lower revenue would be difficult to explain for them. I shared this with my seniors and convinced them that shrinking credit days to 45 days on borrowings of INR 700 million at more than 10% interest rate could yield the business a bottom line of INR 70 million per year. The business was making a small profit after paying for interest in earlier years.

In Nov '93, I was appointed as Vice President Paints responsible for P&L.

Thus, internally, ICI India and Asia Pacific MDs approved our proposal to announce in July a reduction of credit to 45 days from 1 August as the industry practice was.

On 25 July, all sales team was called, and the reason for the reduction of credit days was explained. I felt nobody except a few were convinced, but the implementation of company policy was every employee's responsibility.

As soon as the market was informed of the new credit policy, dealers reacted adversely and stopped taking products from us, while we were running plants to build up stocks for the season.

Normally, each dealer carried a stock of 15-30 days; therefore, their holding power was around 15 days before stocks run out.

The waiting game was on, each passing day worry level shot up by several notches. I continued to reassure as my forecast was based on lots of data from the past and observations about dealers' behaviour. Also, a few loyal dealers had confided in me and encouraged this correction, wanting us to be one of the leaders in the marketplace. Around the tenth day, small orders started trickling in, and by the 29th, we had delivered the full month's supplies.

Everybody in the business was delighted and shared their fears and had difficulty in trusting the decision. While we had the best year in sales and profit, demand was about to outstrip the manufacturing capacity. We had segmented the product range and identified low-cost, low-technology, low-margin products for sourcing out to SME manufacturers

The next step was to find toll converters of quality in Calcutta, Delhi, and Mumbai who could supply low-cost, high-volume products in each region. A QA team was formed and sent out to evaluate various small and medium-scale manufacturers who could deliver on time and in full in the specific region.

This was established in 3 months and this released capacity in the existing two plants and we continued to sell higher than our plant capacity.

At this stage, MD India and MD, Asia Pacific were not definite if this sales growth can be sustained in the medium term and wanted to make sure that it was not a flash in the pan. They wanted to observe a year or two prior to taking a decision to invest funds for a new manufacturing capacity on the West coast.

That year, there was a change of leadership at the top at the CEO, ICI plc level, and he had planned a business visit to India. He spent three days reviewing our past performance of two years and projections for the next two years. The competency to differentiate between high-risk investments and profitable proposals was getting his attention. He was finally convinced that it was the right growth strategy, and we should refine our proposal and prepare for ICI plc Board approval.

6.1   NEW MANUFACTURING FACILITY AT MUMBAI

Once we got the approval to progress, our team got started and also convinced MD India and MD, Asia Pacific. The MD based in Melbourne asked me to get the proposal and back up data and work with him to finalise this presentation. This was finalised in a week's stay at Melbourne, and an appointment was then sought from the secretary of the ICI PLC Board in the UK.

I was asked to present ICI India's Paints business case to the Board on 15 May 1995 for the sanction to install a 20 million-litre plant on existing ICI polyester manufacturing site at Thane-Belapur Road in Mumbai.

I arrived on a Friday for a dummy run at the Millbank-HQ of ICI plc, and the CEO happened to pass by and said it is well written. Half of my nervousness about the uncertainty during the presentation disappeared.

Monday morning, my presentation was the first one at 9 am. I was ushered into the boardroom alone and asked by the Chairman to present my case. As soon as the first slide was presented, there were 3-4 queries, and the Chairman intervened and asked the secretary to write these questions on a flip chart. After the 4th slide, the Chairman answered those questions and said

'Param, your EP is approved.'

Congratulations,'

'Convey our greetings to your team in Calcutta. However, this project should be completed in eighteen months'.

I returned and shared the news of the approval of our project with my colleagues and seniors, highlighting the urgency shown by the Board to complete it in eighteen months' time.

A search was made for engineers of high quality internally and they were assigned to this project. World-class engineering consultants located in India were selected, and a detailed project report was prepared. It took us about three months to develop the construct of the plant as we were bringing some efficient technologies from France and the USA Plants. Our Engineering/HR Director was an outstanding engineer and excellent in organising teams to deliver projects on time. He was guiding the engineering team of this project.

Construction was started and soon we realised that the ground for the plant had rocks underneath. The construction team estimated it could take up to two months to get the surface ready for foundation work to start. This delay was a significant setback for our planning process and could mean, not meeting the deadline of 18 months and thus the failure of our commitment to the management team in the UK.

ICI India also had an explosives manufacturing facility based at Gomia, and the sales team was operating from the head office in Calcutta on the fourth floor, while the Paints team was based on the third floor. I was aware that the explosives R&D team was working on developing micro explosives for specialised usage in mines in India. Since the project was going to be delayed, we were considering all options, and one of them was whether these micro explosives could help in extracting these rocks quickly.

I went and met my counterpart in explosives, and he referred me to their Technical Service Manager. I narrated my dilemma, and he listened to me very patiently. After fifteen minutes, he said, "We have done trials on such terrains, and this could deliver the task." Immediately after that, he mentioned that there would be a price for it, and I left for my project in-charge to negotiate a fair price. An agreement was reached that this part of the project would be under the explosives technical team. Preparation of a suitable explosive for this purpose will take a week, and thereafter, 10 days to complete the task.

I breathed a sigh of relief and hoped that we would catch up on this two-week delay in construction activity later.

Fortunately, the technical team started work urgently and initiated the work early, completing it in 10 days by successfully carrying out micro-blasts to remove the rocky part from the land intended for the construction site.

We had initially planned to work twelve hours per day, but due to this delay, we decided to catch up by working around the clock.

It took some time to gather skilled manpower for this task, and soon we were running well to meet the agreed timelines.

A team to follow-up on suppliers of equipment was appointed and was located in Mumbai, where most of these manufacturers had their manufacturing sites.

This being the latest paints plant for ICI Paints, the best available technologies from France and the USA were incorporated.

It was a highly automated unit and needed one-third of the manpower compared to our older units. These associates were trained for six months and were capable of operating with minimum supervision.

Several times, it was felt that it might not be possible to meet a really challenging time target of 18 months, but we persevered and motivated our team that we are on track and will make it.

Weekly meetings were held at the Mumbai site to review the progress and remove any roadblocks. Suppliers were visited regularly to check if progress was as per the plan. It was a great example of dedicated, result-oriented teamwork and the outstanding leadership of the Director of Engineering and engineers working on-site.

Thus, the plant was commissioned, and regular production was slowly built by pulling out mid-segment products from small manufacturers from whom we were sourcing out in the interim period and participating in growth to improve our market share. We still let low-cost products be supplied by these manufacturers. While the plant was getting production aligned, we thought it is worthwhile to celebrate this event with our seniors in Asia and customers. Thus, a date was decided, and the then Governor of Maharashtra was requested for the opening ceremony. A temporary shaded hall was made to accommodate about 500 people, and after the ceremony, entertainment for visitors and a Rajasthani meal were offered. In the evening, entertainment with local talented artists, etc., was arranged beside a well-spread dinner at The Taj.

After all those celebrations, we got back to business and realised that we have to continue the momentum to achieve above 25% growth YOY, but we will run out of capacity in two years.

Normally, the main segments in the Paints business are as follows, e.g.

1. Decorative
2. Refinish
3. Automotive
4. High Performance

We were running short on refinish paint capacity, and we needed to convince the international refinish business team in the UK for a sanction to build additional capacity. We had a major market share in refinish, and the loss of share could not be ignored.

Simultaneously, we initiated discussions with ICI India management and ICI plc business group. There were misgivings about our request and supporting database; two of the experts visited us to validate our findings. At the end of one week's review, our data was found trustworthy, and this team promised that they will communicate their observations, and we will hear from the CEO, refinish paints. We were informed that the CEO, refinish paints himself wanted to assess the need for this investment and will plan a visit in the next 10 days. We sharpened our presentation, and after two days of questions and answers, he was convinced of the need for expanding the capacity somewhere in the North-West of India.

The CEO was of the opinion that we should have the proposal ready for presentation/approval in the next four weeks. We all put in day and night effort to get the draft ready in two weeks so that the UK business has time to fine-tune for the Board. It was August, and an appointment for presentation to the ICI plc Board in September was requested. I was nominated to present India's case, to the Board. There were several queries that were adequately answered. I also informed the Board that the construction of the decorative EP granted last year, was completed before time, and manufacturing is getting started.

Board members were quite delighted with the timely completion of the Mumbai plant. The Finance Director was so pleased that he said -

'Param, come every year and we will happily clear your 'Expenditure Proposal'

6.2   MANUFACTURING FACILITY IN NORTH-PUNJAB

Our strategy was to have four manufacturing plants located in the East, West, North, and South. Since we already had plants in the East and West, the next location was to be the North.

Thus, a new site in the North was to be evaluated. Rajasthan, Uttar Pradesh, and Punjab were examined for a possible site. In the end, Mohali in Punjab was selected for setting up a refinish/ decorative paints manufacturing unit. It offered a trained result-oriented dedicated workforce, and adequate services e.g. power, water, effluent disposal, etc. The Chief Minister had assured his support and was happy ICI India has decided to invest in Punjab.

This project was more complex as the best practices of French and the US refinish plants were to be incorporated. Engineers needed to visit, study, understand, and obtain the appropriate drawings. The concept was that the first vessel receives the solvent, the vessel moves to the next station and gets all other ingredients, and at the last station, the exact amount of tinters were to be added. The tinters made were of an exact combination, and any deviation will not yield a product of a right colour. At each stage, vigorous stirring was needed, and after a programmed time, the vessel was to move. Normally, no testing was required because the process was so accurate and dependable. The target completion was slated for August 1999.

In summary, between 92-98, the following were major achievements:

1. A world-class team of talented individuals was inducted in each function.
2. Market share tripled.
   Doubled the number of salesmen and dealers in the North-West.
3. We had purchased 10% of Asian paints' shares from one of the owners of Asian paints but could not process it for various reasons.
4. We had launched about four new products in the marketplace which enhanced the top as well as bottom line.
5. Our OTIF improved significantly.
6. We upgraded the capacity at the Hyderabad plant and constructed a new decorative plant at the Mumbai site in 18 months.
7. Got construction started of a new refinish plant at Mohali (near Chandigarh) in the north.
8. Volume growth, trading profit, and net working capital improved substantially. An example is given below:

Volume growth from Year 93 to 94 was +43%.

Trading profit increased from 93 to 94, a rise of 42%.

Net working capital reduced by 39%

It was the best performing year for the Paints business, ICI India at that time. We had the best performing team, and I honestly believed in following John's statement -

> **'80% of a strategy is about the people and the culture because it is the people who create the value.'**
>
> **– John Sunderland, Former CEO, Cadbury**

On a personal front, I was appointed as an ICI Board Member and Executive Director and was also made responsible for the Paints business along with R&D and Marketing functions for all the businesses of the ICI India group.

Chapter-7

Move to Singapore

By 1998, I had completed six years running the Paints business successfully and was to finish my assignment on 31 March 1998. Luckily, I was offered a choice of two-year extension in the present role or a transfer to ICI Asia Pacific Paints located in Singapore, as Regional Director-refinish paints for a period of 5 years. After evaluating all aspects of life, we decided to join the Singapore business on 1st Apr 1998. It was possible since Brunei Airlines had a direct flight early in the morning and we were in Singapore around midday. In the afternoon of 1st Apr 98, there was a Regional Directors's video conference which I was able to attend.

World College of SE Asia was known to be one of the best schools in Singapore, and Shankar, our son, appeared for a written examination for admission to class nine. After the test, we were informed that Shankar qualifies for class ten and not nine, which saved a year and could do IB by 2001.

The role as a Regional Director covered about ten countries, e.g., Indonesia, Singapore, Malaysia, Thailand, China, Hong Kong, Taiwan, and sub-continent. It was a challenging job and required travelling at least 12-15 days a month. Luckily, the airport was close and could be reached in 15-20 minutes. A new learning experience was about understanding the cultures and behaviours in each country as business practices differed in areas such as pricing, inventory management, credit terms, and quality levels, etc.

ICI Paints Asia Pacific had decorative paint manufacturing units in each country, but refinish paints were sourced from Malaysia and the UK. Some countries in Asia had systems and processes, while others had to make a new start. Inducting new talent was a challenge in these countries, and many times we had to select average individuals.

ICI plc was facing a cash crunch and was divesting non-essential portfolios since the early 90s. In the Paints business, the decorative segment was regarded as important, and all other segments of the Paints business were divested to other major paints units worldwide.

The Regional Directors ,refinish business used to have 3-day quarterly review meetings in different places across the globe, and this time, in March 1999, it was being held in Cleveland, Ohio. On the first day of the meeting, the focus was on cost reduction, and each regional director committed to reducing their costs by 5-7% in the following year.

On the second day morning, we were all in the conference room at 8 am, and the Chairman of the meeting was quiet. There was total silence. After 2-3 long minutes, he said-

Gentlemen, I have news for you. Our refinish business has been acquired by PPG of Pittsburgh, and their Vice President would like to meet us at lunch.

There was a pin-drop silence for a few minutes, and then the team had a lot of questions to which the Chairman was in no position to respond. The Vice President of PPG business had driven down from Pittsburgh and took our queries at lunch. They reassured us that the business would grow, there would be small changes over a period of time, and nobody should get alarmed. This team was kept in place for about a year.

The merger was done in a very professional manner, and there were three meetings in Pittsburgh on the smooth transition of the business from ICI plc to PPG Inc. I was informed that since they had no replacement for me, my contract with ICI Paints Asia Pacific will be honoured by PPG Inc., but I have to move to KL where the HQ, Asia will be located.

Since Shankar was in the first year of IB, I requested to allow us to move a year later, in 2001 on completion of the IB course, and that was agreed. After the completion of his IB course, we moved to KL, Malaysia, in June 2001. Shankar decided to join Brandeis University, Waltham, near Boston. This was for a bachelor's degree which he completed in May 2005. He was recruited by E&Y in NY, and he joined them in June 2005.

I continued to work with PPG until March 2003 when my contract term expired.

During my last year of assignment with PPG, I was working on different options, e.g. finding another assignment in Singapore as we were permanent residents and had an offer from the Government of Singapore to convert it into citizenship.

Simultaneously, we were exploring the possibility of starting a management consultancy service. As my family wanted to settle in India rather than Singapore, we needed to focus on the Indian option. Thus, we decided to return to Gurgaon, Haryana, India, where we had an apartment.

Part Two

Chapter-8

Continuous Learning

'We now accept the fact that learning is a
lifelong process of keeping abreast of change.
Knowledge has to be improved, challenged,
and increased constantly or it vanishes.'

– Peter Drucker

'Once you stop learning, you start dying.'

– Albert Einstein

START OF CONSULTANCY SERVICE - 2003

8.1   CONTINUOUS LEARNING

During my career, I was exposed to most of the disciplines required
to run a robust business. For example:

1. Research and Development
2. Production
3. Projects
4. Technical Service
5. Product Development
6. Sales and Purchases
7. General Manager - responsible for the total performance of
   the business

8. Experience of different businesses - Rubber Chemicals, Alkali manufacturing, Plastics, Penta, and Paints including marine paints.

This all-round experience provided me with adequate knowledge to help enterprises with their operations. I was, in a way, a consultant in Singapore and KL as I was advising and mentoring rather than directly involved in any daily operations.

8.2 PROPOSED ACQUISITION OF RUBBER CHEMICALS BUSINESS OF ICI INDIA

It so happened that while I was in KL in March 2003, I was contacted by a business house in Calcutta that was interested in acquiring the Rubber Chemicals business of ICI India. They were aware that I was the GM of that business when I was with ICI India and wanted me to evaluate the profitability of this business and later negotiate with ICI India. There was a cost of acquisition, and the owners were made aware of the possible expenditure.

Rubber Chemicals, when compounded with synthetic or natural rubber, modify its properties like plasticity, elasticity, toughness, hardness, softness, abrasion resistance, etc. Most of these chemicals are used for automotive applications and the rest in hoses, belts, sheets, shoe soles, etc. Three major producers had 60%, and ICI India had about 20% market share. Rubber Chemicals were primarily based on derivatives coming from crude oil; therefore, the price of crude oil had a direct link with the profitability of the business.

A business consultant was required, and Ernst and Young in Delhi was selected and shared the requirement for this task. EY was to collect all the data about the industry, e.g. market size, competition, pricing, channel to the market, etc. EY also needed to prepare a case along with conducting the due diligence. It took us about six months to prepare a case and went ahead with due diligence. About the same time, oil prices virtually doubled in those six months and impacted the profitability. This was because most of the raw materials were based on products from oil origin. We were aware that the tyre industry was highly competitive, and getting a price increase from them is next to impossible. The plant was old and will need a substantial amount to get it running to international standards. Good, productive manpower had already retired, and running hazardous operations with new hands offered additional risk. In view of the main raw material supply depending on international pricing, pricing power with major customers and no substitutes around, we concluded that this is not the most favourable time for acquisition. In view of reduced profitability, it was then decided not to pursue the project any further.

In Oct 03, two small units sought my help to examine how productivity and profitability can be improved. I spent about three months, and in the absence of reliable data, I reached a conclusion that it is not worthwhile to pursue.

8.3 MD – PERSTORP, SWEDEN IN INDIA

In the meantime, in 2005, I received a call from a Hong Kong-based HR group, asking if I would travel to Mumbai to meet the HR Director of Perstorp AB, a chemical unit based in Sweden.

I asked for a day to respond, and with the help of my family and colleagues, I decided to go and meet him.

Perstorp AB was a major player in pentaerythritol, D-Penta, and many other chemicals for the paint, plastic, and explosives industry. They had acquired an Indian Penta manufacturing unit near Mumbai. The parent unit was located in Sweden with a turnover of around a billion Euros.

I had travelled to Mumbai to meet the HR Director of Perstorp AB at Meridien. We had about 3 hours of discussions, and at the end, he asked if, the next Sunday, 10 days from that day, I could be in Copenhagen to meet their Board and the Chairman.

I said that I needed to check with all stakeholders and with one condition, I can operate only from Gurgaon. Besides that, the visa takes time, to which his answer was that we will talk to our embassy in Delhi, and you can get it in 3 days. I flew back to Delhi and discussed whether I should move any further because I was not interested anymore in a 5-days role. The view was that there was no risk to travel to Copenhagen, and therefore arrangements were made appropriately. The meeting was organised in a conference room at Hilton, which was in walking distance of the Copenhagen airport.

At 10 am, I went to the conference room on the first floor of Hilton at the airport and found five senior members of Perstorp AB facing me across the table.

The Chairman explained the role in Perstorp India, which involved full P/L responsibility. Perstorp had their office in Chembur and a plant in Vapi, about 170 km from Mumbai.

I was introduced to all members, and the Chairman said, "We would like to tell you about our issues and evaluate if you could be the right leader to resolve them."

It started out with my educational background and experiences of the industry in India. After an hour's discussion, specific questions were as follows-

1. Process I have used for decision-making
2. Problem solving
3. Man management
4. Commitment to the decisions

Since I had practised all of these at the highest level of operational and strategic level, it was not difficult to respond. After about 3 hours of questions and answers, they had no questions to ask, and the meeting was closed.

The Chairman asked me to join him for lunch, and I agreed. He said, 'Param, you are the right man for the role, but it is a full-time job, and you will have to be in Mumbai.' My answer was that I am not looking for a full-time role and also, I am too costly a person with all the other amenities required. The Chairman said, 'I agree with all your conditions. When can you join?' I was taken aback because I had not expected his agreement. It was a Sunday, and I was leaving the same evening, so I asked for 2 days' time to revert.

I came home on Monday morning and mentioned this proposal, and the response was a clear NO. The reason was that we had just settled in Gurgaon and were getting comfortable with the environment. After a few days of discussions, it was agreed we could go for only a year, and I was in agreement. Within 15 days, we moved to Mumbai and took charge of the organisation. As usual, I met with the Executive members and tried to assess their present and past performances. What were the blocks that did not allow the organisation to grow.

Leadership had not communicated objectives, options, and priorities clearly. There was no clear strategy, and it was more about manufacturing penta and selling imported Perstorp products. In absence of targets, whatever was achieved, was acceptable

The first task for me was to get a strategy for 25% growth year on year approved by the Chairman's team. I had worked on strategy development in my earlier businesses, so it was not so complicated for a smaller business. I was ready in about eight weeks' time, and I informed the Chairman about my readiness.

The Chairman agreed to visit the following week.

Preparations were expedited, and the plant was organised for his visit.

The strategy was presented, and in the end, he was in agreement and asked what support I needed from Sweden. I requested visits of SBU heads quarterly to conduct audits so that we were aligned with their business objectives and meeting agreed targets.

The Chairman wanted me to be in Sweden every 8-10 weeks to brief Board members on the progress made versus the set KRAs.

After my presentation of a "Case for Growth in India"

Board agreed –

1. To expand the market penetration by increasing the dealer network, employing more salespersons, and offering newer products.
2. To expand the capacity of the plant.
3. To provide technical guidance for further improvement of the yield and quality of the product.
4. Organise to separate non-performers and find individuals with a growth mindset.
5. Develop a strong bond with SBU Heads and get support wherever necessary.

Within the following six months, we were cruising towards our goal. Sweden developed confidence and agreed to expand the existing capacity, invest in a Research and Development laboratory, skilled manpower, and installation of a pilot plant for Creosote, a new product for trial and sampling to potential customers in Japan, Korea, and China.

Since my assignment was for a year and I was asked to complete unfinished tasks in an additional three months, I then handed over to a newly appointed Swedish MD who had experience in Asia. After the completion of the MD's role, there was a need for Perstorp AB to prepare a proposal for the "Biofuels market" in India within 6-9 months' time. This I accepted and handled from Gurgaon.

I had hired Frost and Sullivan, Mumbai to help in preparing the case. The findings were submitted in March 2008.

Perstorp AB was undecided about pursuing the project further, so the project was closed.

I had decided to take a six-month break from my consultancy assignments and then it so happened that I received a call on Nov '08 about another assignment in Denmark.

8.4   COUNTRY ADVISER – HEMPEL A/S, DENMARK

In Nov 2008, I received a call from the COO of a Danish paints company, Hempel A/S, who was looking for rapid growth in India and needed a consultant who could help them identify and present a case for expansion / acquisition. In that call, I mentioned that I would operate from Gurgaon but would travel anywhere required for this role.

The COO asked if I could come to Amsterdam and meet their Chairman for a day. I agreed and was with the COO and Chairman and presented possibilities for a Paints business in India. At the end of the day, the Chairman asked if I could join them in a month's time to lead this project for a year.

Hempel's office was based in Mumbai and was reporting to the Head of Asia Pacific located in Singapore. The background of the Indian paints industry was that it was dominated by decorative paints; the ratio between decorative and industrial was 70:30 and was expected to move to an international ratio of 50:50 for the following reasons-

- – Strong growth in underlying sectors such as infrastructure, automobile, consumable durables, etc.
- – strong interest from international players with technical expertise in entering India to leverage the above opportunity.

Both segments, organised and unorganised, had sales of about USD 1.5 BILLION.

Hempel, a billion-dollar company based in Denmark, had a major market share in marine paints worldwide and was looking for an opportunity to expand the market share with a larger customer base.

Since my experience with Frost & Sullivan was good on the Biofuel project of Perstorp AB, I approached them to assist with market research, major players, their strengths and weaknesses in the industry, and possible candidates who could help in expanding the market. The work was initiated in Jan '09, and the base data was built up in about 6 months' time.

Contacts were made with several units, and none was found suitable for the purpose. There was one borderline enterprise, and we explored its suitability, several meetings were conducted to understand-

1. Marketing strategy -
   Product range, pricing, promotion, and channel to the market. This unit was primarily in decorative and some industrial paints segments.
2. Market share, competition, and their strengths and weaknesses in the marketplace vis-a-vis the top 2-3 leaders of the industry
3. Strength of the supply chain — were they able to meet customers' requirements (on time and in full concept - OTIF)
4. Status of manufacturing units and quality standards being met regularly
5. Quality of manpower - adaptable and depth of knowledge in their area of operations
6. Financials - Total sales, costs, and thus net profit after depreciation and interest.
7. Innovations - track record and what is in the pipeline

Total synergy and integration were also considered.

On the face of it, it appeared to be a basket case, but Hempel was looking for an entry into the Indian market.

After getting all the details, we had several discussions internally and agreed to prepare a presentation for the Board. There was a team of three of us - a finance expert from Hempel, the Singapore head for Asia, and me. The conclusion was that the market share was low, costs were high, there was not much of innovation, and the supply chain was poor. It was felt that Hempel would need high investment for the upgradation of this unit, and then only sizeable synergies could be extracted.

A presentation was made by to the Board members of Hempel in Copenhagen. The presentation was smooth and appreciated. However, the Chairman said that we were competing with a proposed acquisition in China, which was found more attractive than India's proposal.

Thus, the project was formally closed in Dec 2009. This project had a one year tenure, and I was happy to be a part of it.

8.5   COUNTRY ADVISER – DULUX AUSTRALIA

In January 2010, I received a request to meet one of the senior members of Dulux Australia who was visiting Mumbai on business. It was a day's visit, so the meeting was set up around 11 AM.

I met the GM-Strategy, and he shared Dulux's interest in developing options for the entry of one of their product ranges in India. Since I had to operate from Gurugram, I agreed to his proposal.

The project timeline to complete was 18-24 months.

I returned to Gurgaon and initiated a search for a suitable consultant in Delhi itself. One of the referrals was "Feedback Consultants," and I had to ascertain their capability of conducting this type of project within the given financial limits and timelines.

Several discussions were held with Feedback Consultants and found them quite suitable to carry out this project. 'Feedback' allocated two consultants for this work since they had experience of market research in the field of paints and adhesives.

The remit given to them was –

1. Is it possible to import products from their overseas plant to seed the market?
2. Would there be a case to set up a manufacturing facility in India?
3. If there is a candidate worthy of acquisition.

Timeline: 18-24 months

There was monitoring every fifteen days by me and every two months by the territory manager based in Malaysia.

Market research findings were available within three months and a review was planned along with the territory manager. Market visits and entities for possible collaboration or acquisition were identified. Market visits were made and surveys conducted about the brand in India. We visited around ten small units and did not find any suitable unit.

The problem was that small units cared less about hygiene, safety, health, and the environment, and sometimes quality. There was a small enterprise near Delhi, and we evaluated the possibility of using their channel. A visit to his manufacturing unit was made, and we found the same issues as mentioned earlier. The site had poor engineering standards, there was little concern for people's safety, quality control was non-existent, financials were poorly recorded and appeared to be inaccurate in some places. If we had gone ahead, it would have required major expenditure, reducing the viability of the project. Prices were kept low in order to compete with small enterprises, So the sales value was higher but with low profitability.

There is the major enterprise holding major market share and leader for several years. It was felt to test out if their channel could be utilised for launching this product line.

An appointment was sought and meeting held where details of the proposal were discussed.

It was agreed to evaluate the possibility in next few weeks so that a view can emerge. Since products were DIY and still have not gained ground in India the product offer was unsuitable at this point of time.

Thus, it was decided not to pursue any further, and the project was closed. This was my last international consultancy, in 2011.

Part Three

Chapter-9

Support to Small, Medium Enterprises – India

'OUR SMALL HAND TO MAKE YOU LARGE.'

– Ministry of SMEs

I was tired of travelling and full-time involvement in any activity. After I had finished my projects with international enterprises, I looked at SMEs in India that were hungry for growth and were looking for the right part-time help.

9.1   BACKGROUND OF MSMES

India is one of the fastest-growing economies and has the third-largest number of family businesses in the world.

There are several hundreds of examples where 30-year-old companies are crossing the INR 1,000 crores annual revenue mark. India has 271 billionaires out of a total of 3279 worldwide, and about 110 families account for a trillion USD output.

MSMEs account for 30% of India's GDP, 40% of the national industrial production, and 42% of total exports.

Number of MSMEs in India is about 63 million, out of which 96% are micro. About 90% of the total industrial units employ 120 million, 40% of India's workforce. The distribution of SMEs is:

31% in manufacturing, 36% in trade, and the rest in other sectors.

Fifty-one percent exist in rural areas and 49% in urban areas.

Entrepreneurs have different mindsets, and attempts have been made to segment them because each one could have a different approach. Some of these are listed below-

1. Innovators-

Who comes up with completely new ideas & turns them into viable businesses.

2. Go-Getters

Work very hard and many times, hands-on.

They start small but with a goal in mind to become large and are very focused and take risks in the short term. It takes longer for them to achieve, and the chances of success are lower.

3. Imitators-copy

There are some existing business ideas and they improve upon them.

These enterprises look for improvement in the product offer. Normally, they are a mix of the first two types and have a lot of self-confidence.

4. Explorers / Researchers-

Even after having an idea worked out, they will continue to explore to the last detail from all angles. The chances of success are higher.

5. Buyers.

These entrepreneurs have funds, identify a business, assess its viability, and proceed to acquire and find the most suitable person to run it.

Despite being an 'engine of growth', the sector struggles on various fronts like timely financial support, technological obsolescence, higher cost of production in some segments, and tough competition in the international market. Some issues are discussed later.

I had 2-3 small businesses pursuing me to be their mentors. These were entrepreneurs who had little experience of running an organisation on professional lines.

The corporate culture of these units was based on their beliefs, practices, and perception of the world and was normally founded by the owner/entrepreneur.

There was ad-hoc decision-making and running the business more by interventions wherever there was a roadblock. There were very few written systems and procedures which were used to yield a consistent quality of output.

Entrepreneurs who are driven by the idea of winning and view everything in terms of immediate success miss a broader medium-term perspective, as they do not realise that pursuing a longer-term perspective could be a more beneficial option. Entrepreneurs are passionate about pursuing something they regard as unique, confident of success, and have a high capacity for risk. These are hardworking, highly motivated individuals with the ability to make decisions even with incomplete data. These competencies normally lead them to a revenue level of INR 50-100 crores. (Ref. 6)

Some, who had a desire to grow faster than the market growth rate and believed that what they did in the entrepreneurial stage of the business could be extended to achieve doubling the business revenue over a period of time were unsuccessful.

These family businesses were not able to succeed using the past practices because of the size, complexities, and uncertainties faced in a larger business. The founder, along with his loyal, highly committed team, could not pull off and felt exhausted and helpless. They wanted to grow but could not figure out how to manage expanded chaos.

9.2 PROBLEMS OF GROWTH

Successful enterprises had outstanding people and formed extraordinary teams to deliver results, better than the competition. Many of the small & medium enterprise owners regarded people as costs and many times could not afford high compensation packages operating in the market.

While on this subject, Jim Collins tried to resolve this dilemma.

'As a company grows and becomes more complex, it begins to trip over its own success - too many customers, too many new orders, too many new products. What was great fun becomes an unwieldy ball of disorganised stuff. Lack of planning, lack of accounting, lack of systems, and lack of hiring constraints create friction. Problems surface - with customers, cash flow, with schedule.' (Ref-3)

So, in the absence of systems and procedures, most of the decisions were taken on a gut-feel basis, and some decisions were right while some were not. It was difficult to figure out whose responsibility it was for an incorrect decision, or a substandard batch made in the factory.

The concept of mentors or consultants was taking roots in India, and each one was looking for an outside knowledge source that could upgrade their functions and recommend how to be more professional and grow faster than the market growth rate.

I had contacts in the industry; the first two were from the cosmetic and pharma units. I spent a few months and found out that there were conflicts within the owners' family which appeared to be irreconcilable. I communicated with the parties and I discontinued working with them.

Next two were Pharma enterprises, these were better organised but had issues with the owner unwilling to pass on authority to the next generation. Family-owned companies are more than 80% in India, and many have issues within the family. Some sought professional help and sorted out legacy issues amicably. Others had long-drawn court cases, and some were settled, and some were not.

I selected units that were ethical and hungry for growth. Once an agreement was reached, a roadmap was drawn, and views on investment in machines, skilled manpower, and technology were clearly defined with timelines. There were two Senior Managers assigned as leaders for the upgrading work, and I would spend a few days a week to help them plan and execute in line with the overall objective of getting systems and procedures implemented.

Management was briefed on the drastic changes regarding a possible shift from gut-feel decision-making to a data-based approach in the day-to-day life of the business.

9.3   PHARMA INDUSTRY

There are about 8000 drug companies with a likely turnover of $45bn. There are about 750 USFDA approved units, and many EUGMP and MHRA approved units.

The unit I got associated with was a small one but with the potential to grow several times in future. I was also keen to see if my professional approach to large units was applicable to small units and if it would take root to grow. There was a detailed discussion about the process followed by a well organised enterprise The first step was to decide to what is the organisations goal. Once that was agreed, it was possible to develop a preliminary strategy for the business, which was realistic and doable. It is useful to remind your goal so that organisation does not get off course. Lewis's quote is very appropriate and thus emphasis on the goal first.

'If you do not know where you are going, any road will get you there.'

– Lewis Carroll

We started with a full audit of each function, and the SWOT clearly indicated the gaps and allowed to construct a roadmap for developing a sound strategy. Unfortunately, very few records were available from the past on the basis of which one could build the template for a futuristic strategy.

My work with one of the units is described below. The issues of the other units were very similar and thus not repeated.

When you initiate a journey, it is important to have your compass to determine your direction and keep you on track vis-a-vis the set-out goal. Similarly, it is crucial for stakeholders to deeply introspect and decide what their vision, values, and desired culture are. Some details were outlined-

9.4   VISION, VALUES, AND CULTURE

One needs to define the vision for which you need to identify the kind of prevailing culture vs. the desired one and values which got inculcated through the owner/entrepreneur.

Values represent the core of who you are. They not only influence your life but that of the whole organisation. Like your moral judgement, the people you trust, the appeals you respond to, and the way you invest your time and money. One of the important values like trust, if built between owners and operators, then in difficult times, the workforce supports with full commitment because of the connection developed by the management.

Susan Fowler (2017) described Values as follows:

"Values are predetermined, logical standards of what a person considers good or bad, worse, better, or best." Having chosen to accept these guidelines.

Values are at the heart of high-quality self-regulation, yet most individuals have not explored their own work-related values.

– Individuals need to identify, develop, clarify, declare and operationalise their own work-related values and purpose and then determine how they align with the organisation's "values."

Values are guiding principles of a person or of an enterprise.

Some examples of values demonstrated are given below-

1. Truthfulness; transparency in dealings, and no hidden agenda
   "Do what you say"
   Honesty, integrity, being factual
2. Unselfishness, kindness, compassion, empathy
3. Teamwork
4. Gratitude, helping others, guiding, mentoring
5. Self-control, free from arrogance, envy and hatred

In today's world, these values receive much less attention primarily because people are engaged in fulfilling their materialistic needs rather than value-based needs. The mismatch between laid-out values and those followed could be one of the reasons for most people's dissatisfaction.

9.5 CORPORATE CULTURE

Corporate culture usually means values, beliefs and practices that are shared across all groups in the company.

It has been observed that many times these family businesses were not able to succeed using the past practices because of the size, complexities, and uncertainties faced in a larger business. Studies on corporate culture show that-

a) Corporate culture can have a significant impact on the long-term economic performance of the enterprise. The units that focused on customers and employees with quality leadership from managers performed better than unfocused organisations.

b) Performance-degrading cultures have a negative impact on financial outcomes as there is a tendency to inhibit enterprises from strategic and tactical changes from time to time.

c) Although tough to change, corporate culture can be made to be more performance oriented. Such change is complex, takes time, and requires leadership. (Ref-12).

The owner, entrepreneur, along with his loyal, highly committed team with some knowledge of modern management concepts, cannot pull off and feels overwhelmed.

The culture built by them was an owner-driven organisation. This emerges over time from the vision of the owner/leaders which requires a set of behaviours to deliver the vision.

In the absence of organisational vision, it is possible that sub-groups could develop their own understanding and communicate it as the organisation's vision. At times, it could deliver results that are not aligned with corporate objectives and later will need realignment. The culture needs to be reviewed from time to time and should be capable of adapting to changes in the environment.

It is known that a business cannot be "renewed" without changing behaviours. Sometimes it is perceived as "attitudinal change", which is unlikely to change as adults very rarely change their fundamental attitude. Thus, there exists a dilemma as to how to renew the business, which needs changing people's mindset. It is possible to change behaviour without changing the attitude. The real challenge of changing behaviour is then to change the context around the people by the new leadership.

There was no vision statement; therefore, first a vision and values for the enterprise were drawn with the collaboration of stakeholders. Once finalised, they were communicated to all down the line.

On the basis of the above, the foundation of a productive cultural shift was designed.

All functions were audited, inadequacies were established, and follow-up actions were instituted. Some are described below-

9.6   SALES AND MARKETING

The enterprise had a dozen major customers and the rest were all small dealers/wholesalers scattered all over Asia and Africa.

There were managers who looked after these countries and the main customers directly dealt with by the owner. The owner's son had come back after an MBA from the USA and had a lot of ideas about the way the business can be reorganised.

A detailed search was made in Asia and Africa to identify suitable dealers/wholesalers. Some responded, and those leads were progressed and concluded.

While systems were being put in place, the major customer based in Europe and supplying different parts of the world, according to new regulations, was required to receive supplies only from EU GMP-approved units from India.

This required a major change in the way business was running to meet WHO GMP guidelines. An adviser was appointed to identify EU GMP guidelines for implementation. A local experienced adviser was sought and brought in to instil the right culture to comply with EU GMP systems.

Extensive training was organised for all levels of workers to communicate what changes will be required to meet new regulations.

Employees were made aware of the importance of customers for the business. In a highly competitive environment, customer satisfaction is of prime importance. The sales team was to brief customer feedback each month so that some of the suggestions could be implemented. Customer-centric leadership was aware that customers must be treated well, and their needs attended to on high priority as growth potential will depend on our delighted customers.

On the basis of sales forecast received from the customers; production planning was designed. This led to requirements for raw materials and packaging materials, which were decided upon by purchasing team after negotiating the price and delivery periods.

The product mix was re-examined, and products with lower value in the last 3 years, and customers with a complicated product mix and lower sales, were informed about discontinuation after 6 months. Most of them agreed to this change.

An in-depth study was undertaken about product life cycles, new product introduction plan, territories for existing products, and new products in existing and new markets, and decisions were implemented. Sales personnel were appointed responsible for specific countries and meeting sales and collection targets on time.

9.7 MIGRATION FROM WHO TO EUGMP CERTIFICATION

There was a request from the European customers that after the end of this year, they will be required to purchase products only from EUGMP-approved manufacturing units outside Europe.

It was possible to set up EU GMP standards for a manufacturing facility, but the real challenge was to meet the difficult quality standards set by these international approving authorities. Many times, these units also hired some of the best talent in manufacturing but still were unable to qualify to those standards. A lot of work was done to establish the reasons, and it was felt that training the employees in manufacturing was the key to being a quality company. However, this alone did not offer consistency in product quality and many times failed when a scrutiny of the systems was done.

Much later, behavioural scientists found that it is really the attitude of the people towards quality compliance, and many had a casual approach since they were not aware or did not feel motivated to follow a disciplined mindset required to meet those requirements.

It was realised that all who are engaged in the manufacturing activity needed a "Quality Mindset."

Some units felt that if strict discipline was implemented, it could bring the desired results, while some launched technical training programmes. All these experiments brought some improvement in compliance but did not yield a total process for full compliance.

Our analysis indicated that the top level of employees were quite aware of the significance of quality in the system, but the doers at the bottom half either were not aware or did not want to follow since it was too cumbersome for them.

Therefore, the way forward was to put in a disproportionate amount of effort to initiate a cultural change, which takes more time but could be sustainable in the long-term.

It also required accurate documentation work of the past several years. QC and QA systems were reorganised as per those guidelines. The layout needed to be modified, and a cultural shift was necessary to supply a quality product as per EU GMP. Staff and workers had to be trained in HR, workplace hygiene, and following SOPs, BMRs, and BPRs. The migration from WHO GMP company to EU GMP required a total transformation, which appeared to be a near-impossible task in a shorter timeframe. Experienced consultants, experts in the workings of EU GMP operations, were searched for and appointed

Internal teams of competent managers were formed to examine the suitability of earlier data and the addition of accurate new data meeting EUGMP requirements. They worked very hard and were able to complete the tasks within the timeframe.

Equipment: minor modifications were carried out with new investments by engineering.

Finally, a date for inspection was requested, and one was granted after 3 months. They had conveyed their requirements, and which were to be complied prior to the inspection. The duration of the inspection was 4-5 days.

The inspection was exhaustive, and some minor observations were made during the 5-day inspection. On the fifth day afternoon, they read out their observations and once those conditions were complied with, they agreed to issue the EUGMP certification within three months.

Everyone was delighted.

9.8   FINANCE

Most of the SMEs started by entrepreneurs who knew the unmet demand of the consumer with the financial support of the extended family. They worked very hard with very few people and faced issues such as getting raw materials and packing material in time, quality issues because of untrained manpower, and many times customers not accepting material as they were holding stocks for a month or two. There were some medium-sized customers who would delay payments since they had difficulty in managing their own cash flow. They were in a fix, facing a large customer for timely payment. Stopping supplies meant losing business to the competition, and continuing the business meant more borrowings and reduced bottom line.

In many industries, it is common to delay payments for stretched working capital requirements of their own enterprise. Up to a certain scale, the owner does not like to borrow from banks or outside agencies, which is now gradually changing, and owners are finding loans from financial institutions essential for rapid growth.

9.9   HR STRATEGY

> **'80% of a strategy is about the people and the culture because it is the people who create the value.'**
>
> **– John Sunderland, Former CEO, Cadbury**

In the absence of a strategy, these ambitious entrepreneurs gradually kept growing until they ran out of plant capacity. Issues with family-owned enterprises were that they had very few trustworthy, quality-minded staff left as attrition rates were high. It was difficult to find capable manpower at the workers' level, and they required quite exhaustive training and experience.

There was no people management system. People were hired when needed and released when not required. Only a few loyal all-rounders were on the permanent payroll.

These temporary hires were inexperienced and had no concept of quality standards. This seemingly gave a sense of increased productivity, but rejects were much higher.

Successful enterprises have outstanding people and form extraordinary teams to deliver results better than the competition. Small & medium owners regard people as costs and many times cannot afford them in the market.

Jim Collins addresses the human resource dilemma as follows:

'The good to great leader understands three simple truths. First, if you begin with "who" rather than "what", you can more easily adapt to a changing world. If people join the bus primarily because of where it is going, what happens if you get ten miles down and you need to change direction? You have got a problem. But if people are on the bus because of who else is on the bus, then it is much easier to change the direction.'

Second, if you have the right people on the bus, the problem of how to motivate and manage the people largely goes away.

Third, if you have the wrong people, it does not matter whether you discover the right direction; you still will not have a great company. Great vision without great people is irrelevant.' (Ref-4)

In order to correct this gap, an HR manual was prepared in consultation with seniors in the business, and appropriate communications were made. A performance management system was introduced. A training calendar was drawn up based on the needs identified by the managers.

The importance of integrity at work was crucial, and the workforce was made aware of keeping it in mind all the time during operations.

Knowledge about EHS and engineering standards was non-existent. An experienced person was hired and asked to draw up plans to bring the unit up to date.

9.10 DECISION-MAKING

In the entrepreneurs' / family-owned businesses, the decision-making rests with one or two seniors. This management style was demotivating to line management and inhibited innovation, teamwork, and the responsibility of their actions in assigned roles.

The decision-making can be of two kinds - reversible and irreversible. Reversible kinds are taken every day and, in an ad, -hoc manner. However, irreversible ones require the definition of the need, what will it yield as the bottom line, who are the manufacturers, price, and time of delivery. A thorough process should be written down and followed by all the seniors who identify the need. Financial authorities could be passed down depending on the level of work. (Ref. 6)

In the eyes of the staff and workers, the top exists to control by rigid HR rules and create a tight reporting system.

In case managers have not made some connections, there is always a feeling of dissatisfaction. Small issues of their's remain unresolved while HR is busy in firefighting instead of upgrading performance of the people

What is not realised is that larger units put reliable procedures and systems in place and nurture a competent team of leaders who will gradually understand the business nuances and will implement these appropriate systems successfully.

9.11 PRODUCTIVITY

There was no forecast for the month, so occupancy was as low as 30%. Batch sizes were small, so the cost of production was high.

Each time a product change was needed, some machine components had to be changed, cleaning times and testing times were longer. This was the main reason for lower productivity. During this period, the product had to be held in the Quarantine area until cleared by the analytical laboratory. Each raw material and other additives needed to be tested as per specification. Integrity while testing is another issue that the industry is facing today. All these factors yielded low productivity of the machine and manpower.

Some customers held smaller stocks; thus, there were often more repeat orders with high urgency. Customers wished for supplies to be made within 30 days, while some raw materials' delivery time was 20 days. Inventory management was need-based, and key raw materials were either in small quantities or missing. The maintenance of buffer quantities for fast moving items was not practised. This impacted the planning and the promised delivery date to the customer.

9.12 INNOVATION

Another issue faced was that founders felt that their way of operations was the best way, and any change could be unreliable and full of uncertainties. With time, many had lost the spirit of innovation.

So, with no innovation in the product range, old equipment, a loyal unproductive workforce, and unreliable customers, the business was static or indicating a downward trend. Since many were not strategic thinkers, it was difficult to figure out "how to grow". Some who had been successful wanted to grow at a faster rate than that of the market growth rate. But they had realised that the approach taken initially as an entrepreneur is unlikely to succeed and were looking for help that could lead them to rapid growth.

In order to accelerate product development a small product development group was set up initially with eight scientists and expanded as the advantages were visible to the management. Not only did the quality of existing products improve, but 4-5 new molecules could be brought to the market simultaneously in many countries. After three years, when sales and profits were higher, the owners thought of expanding it. This was a game-changer as contract manufacturers wanted to develop products and also to provide subsequent supplies of these products.

"Though I was trained as a research scientist, my passion lies with people and culture. My motivation lies in trying to figure out how to make the team better and find new solutions to old problems. We keep challenging ourselves to figure out which problem to solve next, how to collaborate better, be more productive, and always raise the bar for team collaboration to achieve better outcomes." (Ref. 13)

Albert Einstein once said:

He had no special talent but was rather passionately curious. It sparks new levels of creativity in your work, observe things around you and demands to step out of your comfort zone.

People with a 'higher curiosity quotient' - CQ are more inquisitive and generate more original ideas, and this unorthodox style of thinking leads to high levels of knowledge learning. This could be a way to produce simple solutions to complex problems.' (Ref. 14)

9.13   CUSTOMER FOCUSED ENTERPRISE

In old businesses, customers were few and had friendly relationships. Quality or price could be compromised on the strength of their familiarity. However, in today's world, competition is acute, pricing is a major issue, and supplies on time are a must. Therefore, as part of the cultural shift, each individual has to be sensitised about the importance of a customer and their needs. From the receptionist to a shop floor operator, it was explained why customers are crucial to the growth of the company. Several training programmes were conducted and repeated every week. Steps taken to improve quality were yielding results, and with customer focused delivery of the products, they were on time and in full. Complaints or enquiries from customers were attended to on high priority. Thus, customer satisfaction increased each year, and customer complaints were close to zero.

Chapter-10

Quality of Leadership
Role of Authentic Leadership in Working Life

> '**The best way to lead people into
> the future is to connect with
> them deeply in the present.**'
>
> **– James M. Kouzes and Barry Z. Posner**

One of the basic principles I held on to was 'Do what you say'. Share frankly the situation and communicate what is relevant to the situation and no more. If something was not within the authority, I shared but promised to pass it on to higher-ups. In working life, one gets time to interact with seniors, colleagues, and the workforce so that one could build a good connection. Truth is the only basis to be an authentic leader.

In actual life, we carry two thoughts simultaneously, one is not shared, and the other one is shared with the workforce and colleagues. At times, this duplicity of what we say and what we do is noted by people around us. They are unlikely to comment but internally will not trust you. We might assume these people would not remember, but most of them do. This does not allow sustainable long-term connection. In my experience, an authentic leader succeeds many times more than the other kind. It is a mindset whether you wish to be truthful or untruthful and that guides the future of each differently. I have experienced both kinds and decided to practice being a truthful leader. The following is a detailed explanation about this kind of leadership.

10.1   EMPHATHETIC LEADERSHIP

Before you can lead others, you must lead yourself and believe that we can have a positive impact on others. We must believe that our words can inspire, and our actions can motivate others. We must believe that what we do count for something. If I do not, you will not even try. Leadership begins with us. {Ref. 12}

Authenticity develops through growth, and growing as a leader requires how well your empathetic relationship is with the workforce. Empathy is about experiencing what others are thinking or feeling. To build credibility by doing what you say.

People engage with trust and want to associate with leaders who are authentic. We can be a better person of ourselves at work if we believe in these values and practices and develop them as a second habit.

Change does not come from the environment we are working in; change begins with us, no matter our age or our size. Many times, the trigger is one event which to others looks small but for some individuals could be a life-changing event. Most journeys start this way, with simple motivation and a choice to do something or not. The decision you take can be right or wrong, but we alone face the consequences. (Ref. 15)

10.2   'ASK IT SHALL BE GIVEN'

Steve Jobs 'called up Bill Hewlett (Co-founder of Hewlett-Packard) when he was 12 years old and said, "I am a student in high school. I want to build a frequency counter, and I was wondering if you have any spare parts I could have." He laughed and gave him the spare parts and offered him a job that summer at Hewlett-Packard — and he was in heaven.

This is the 'power of ask'. The same can be said about the workplace where people are reluctant to ask for help, and I have many times counselled to seek help as nobody is obliging anybody else. We are working to fulfil the enterprise's goal. In many businesses today, they hesitate and feel ego gets hurt.

The power of 'ASK' is limitless, and if colleagues ask for solutions from experts in other functions, the organisation's goals can be achieved in a shorter time.

For example, I had a problem with the rocky land we got for the paints plant at CAFI Site on Thana-Belapur Road. To level it manually, it would have taken an extra two months. I thought of seeking help from the explosives business as I had heard that they had developed micro explosives which were used in mines.

Initially I was hesitant, but my experience came to the fore and advised it's no harm. I did and benefited immensely.

So, asking for help from each other where expertise exists should be encouraged and asked. It helps the individual and the enterprise. I found difficulty in the initial period but as I moved learning 'critical information seeking competency', I found it very useful. It is though hard to practice but if one can take out that fear then the individual and the organisation succeed.

It is easier to communicate what would be a desirable behaviour, but the real impact is only when the workforce observes if this behaviour is being practised by the senior leadership. Some of the aspects of authentic leadership are described below-

10.3   SOLVING PROBLEMS AND DECISION-MAKING

The process that precedes decision-making is problem solving, where information is gathered, analysed, and considered. This is deceptively difficult to get right, yet it is a key input into decision-making for major issues as well as daily ones (such as how to handle a team dispute). Also, taking responsibility for one's actions and decisions is a hallmark of strong leadership. It culminates in a culture of trust and reliability across the enterprise.

As an example, my presentation was ready for the expansion of capacity at CAFI Site to ICI plc Board, a senior sales manager sought an appointment at 8 pm (my flight was at 12:30 from Calcutta) and said, "You are building additional capacity, and there is inadequate demand, and competitors are also in the process of putting up capacity. I urge you to abandon this project." He gave his logic for an hour, and then I was getting late, so I concluded by thanking him for letting me know his views.

The process of decision-making is complex, and normally there are a lot of views outside the business. I, as the leader of the business, had to reconfirm and move ahead as I thought our assumptions were right.

10.4 OPERATING WITH A STRONG RESULT ORIENTATION

Leadership is about not only developing and setting objectives but also following through to achieve results.

Having a clear vision and articulating it down the line inspires and motivates the workforce. The accountability and responsibility can be clearly assigned down the line by communicating a vision and a system to monitor progress every month or quarterly could be introduced.

In the Paints business within a year, we had a dynamic young team with immense energy. We got together in Kathmandu and spent three days to get the preliminary strategy for the business out.

The biggest gain was that there was total alignment to the goal and each one took responsibility for their roles.

10.5 SEEKING DIFFERENT PERSPECTIVE

Leaders with a strong results orientation tend to emphasise the importance of efficiency and productivity and to prioritise the highest-value work. This requires a growth mindset and hard work. Nothing ever comes to one that is worth having, except as a result of hard work.

Example - We were short on capacity in Paint Plants. After a brainstorming session, it was agreed that we should source out low-value, high-volume products to free up some capacity in existing plants. It worked for two years, and by then we had our own capacity. Normally, we did not source out because of technology leakage, but for low-technology, low-cost products, it was accepted. This view led to a conclusion to source out and generate additional capacity in existing plants.

This trait is present in creative, experienced leaders who monitor environmental and business trends affecting organisations. Leaders who do well on this dimension typically base their decisions on sound analysis and avoid many biases to which decisions are prone. These are data-based and not on gut-feel.

10.6   SUPPORTING OTHERS

Leaders who are supportive understand and sense how other people feel. By showing authenticity and a sincere interest in those around them, they build trust and inspire and help colleagues to overcome challenges. They intervene in group work to promote organisational efficiency, allaying unwarranted fears about external threats and preventing the energy of employees from dissipating into internal conflicts.

Example: Our Paints business team was virtually new, but goal setting was realistic. There was a high degree of appreciation of each other's strengths, thus a high level of trust was built up, and we believed that the goal could be achieved.

Chapter-11

What are the Learnings

> **'Control your own destiny or someone else will.'**
>
> **– Jack Welch**

The analysis of my decisions and their impact on the business taught me many aspects of running a business profitably. I was lucky to work with outstanding leaders, and some of their characteristics were identified, which I tried to inculcate. I was always keen to find out why each of us did things the way we did. That reasoning emerged from interactions with many people from different countries and their business practices. Experience tells us that our behaviours with colleagues and fellow workers are more important than having highly sophisticated machines, robust systems, and procedures. In one organisation with state-of-the-art equipment, output remained poor. The main reason discovered was less attention to the needs of the workforce, a disconnect between the management and the operators, and thus highly demotivated teams.

It is the outstanding people who build great organisations.

Some of my learnings related to sound management practices and behaviours are described below. -

11.1   PLANNING

Plan well for any activity you are engaged in.

Most of us are action-oriented and rush into making things happen. Our strategic thinking takes the back seat, and many times we select the wrong path because of a lack of considering strategic implications. If we all plan our day, week, and month, our efficiency will go up substantially.

> **'If you fail to plan, you are planning to fail.'**
>
> **– Benjamin Franklin**

11.1 Do not be afraid of getting your hands dirty and do not outsource important work to a third party or a junior who may not understand the rationale behind the task's importance, what needs to be observed, and what actions need to be taken, if necessary.

e.g. I participated with the workforce wherever a new trial was being undertaken, sometimes continuously for 48 hours. For example, autoclave installation.

11.2 Not to be fearful about committing a mistake. That is the only way one learns. Under such circumstances, some people will make an adverse remark, and one must learn to cope with it. Do not get discouraged and plan your next step with higher energy and enthusiasm. This is how you become a 'Fearless Leader'.

11.3 Learn to deal with the workforce with respect and try to understand, and sometimes anticipate, the workforce's needs in advance.

a) If these needs are minor in nature, take action before they express their demand, for example, providing them with a water cooler.

11.4 You learn more by attentive learning than just giving a long speech to show "how smart a person I am". Listening develops a bond where an individual is likely to trust you. Listening is very important to develop a connection between your people and yourself. If you achieve that breakthrough, you demonstrate empathy and if you correct the grievance speedily, you are regarded as an authentic leader.

11.5 There will always be setbacks in a journey, and one must have a mindset to convert adversity into an opportunity. One must always have Plan B worked out in case Plan A fails. The industry rarely appreciates failures but mostly wants successes.

11.6 There must be a total commitment to the task if only success is desired. Besides learning, hard work and more hard work are required. If one is fearful, the chances of progressing up the ladder are low.

11.7 **Strategy**

A strategist should be able to differentiate between relevant and irrelevant issues. A strategist needs to have a broader vision of what could be likely scenarios in three to five years. It involves scanning likely environmental positions, future changes likely to take place in technology, and any likely disruptive developments which can impact the business. This should result in a sound strategy for the business, including all functions.

The first step is a strategy for the business, and the bottoms-up approach starts from the demand side of the market. On one side, you collate the total market demand, and on the other side, costs of different functions must be matched for a desired gross margin. If it is not in line, one of the factors will need adjustment. Expenditure on capital investment needs to be decided as per the need of the business. Goal setting is crucial because if an error is made at this stage, all follow-up work will get vitiated.

Following are some of the very helpful concepts that I had studied and applied frequently to arrive at the right result. There were a few mistakes which were regarded as learning experiences and noted so that these are not repeated. The quality of decision-making continued to improve and took less time.

For example:

   a)   Goal setting.
   b)   Self-Discipline - it is a must for running a successful enterprise.

c) Mindset and its relationship with culture.

d) Understanding of competencies – many of them have been used throughout the book.

Goals are designed with the intent that they will be accomplished within a stipulated time frame. The success would depend on how deeply your people are committed to the goal. It also depends on the credibility of the leader. It takes time to demonstrate your credibility, not once but several times until people working with you have built up trust. This would mean you will deliver what you say. In today's world, we all get segregated, and only candidates who perform consistently are gradually recognised as the potential leaders of the future.

When I was GM - chemicals business, for two years we delivered exactly what we had forecasted. It certainly was the result of a good strategy and hard work of the team but also an element of luck.

These results were regarded as an extraordinary performance which created some doubts in the minds of leaders at ICI plc of which I was unaware. ICI plc sent an auditor to test if these results are real and report back if these achievements were correct.

After a month, I was asked to meet this gentleman. After a brief introduction, he confided that his purpose of the visit was to audit our results, but he could not find anything irregular so 'Congratulations, Param, for a good performance of your team.'

Once this credible finding was in the system, there was help from all quarters. The long-pending need for a manufacturing plant for antiozonants was sanctioned. A Board Director of ICI plc helped us to get the technology required for this project.

In my experience, setting an objective for the business is crucial. It takes into account not only your internal situation but also the environment, including Government policies that can impact your goal. I have emphasised a little more on the process of goal setting.

> **'Goal setting is the secret to a compelling future. Setting goals is the first step in turning the invisible into visible.'**
>
> **– Tony Robbins**

11.2 GOAL SETTING

11.2.1 Importance of Goal setting-

Your ambition is to achieve your purpose, your dream. Desire motivates action and also creates a void which, when filled, gives you that desired result.

The goal is to achieve what you want. It is important to ponder on your goal of the present and possibly the future, especially something about which you are passionate.

A goal is a desired outcome of an action or task. The value of goal setting is that it helps you to take the unclear idea and turn it into a reality. Setting a goal and working out steps to achieve it accomplishes many things in life.

For example, when we were running our Paints Plants at full capacity, a decision about investment had to be made. We had the following options:

1. Optimise the present resources
2. Test out if lower segment products could be sourced
3. Invest in the most appropriate location for the business - West or North
4. Import and sell
5. Do nothing

Out of these first three choices, two were worth consideration.

Once the goal is clear, then implementation is required.

The criterion of **Goal Setting** should be as follows:

1. The goal should be bordering on possible and impossible - a stretch goal - but is doable. It should be realistic considering the prevailing environment or likely to be in the future. You need to introspect to figure out a 3-year vision for the enterprise and what you would like to see the company achieve in the next 3 years. The entrepreneur/owner should define what is a stretchable goal for the organisation. It should be ensured that it is aligned with the vision, culture, and values.

> **'A person without a purpose is like a ship without a rudder.'**
>
> **– Thomas Carlyle**

The following process is one of the well-established processes to test out if the goal is meaningful and relevant.

George Doran first used the S.M.A.R.T. acronym in the Nov. 1981 issue of Management review. It stands for Specific, Measurable, Attainable, Relevant, and Time-bound. These are briefly explained below-

11.2.2   Goal should be specific-

A general statement will not allow you to set a goal that is attainable. You need to define what is needed within a specific timeframe to achieve that goal. So, the first step is to identify your goal in the near term, say one year to three years. You need to conclude your thought process by writing down your 'inner self' position, prioritising different suggestions, and doing a SWOT analysis (strengths, weaknesses, opportunities, and threats). Once a goal is clearly defined, the rest is to make it a reality through our teams.

11.2.3   Goal should be measurable-

It is postulated that one should not undertake work that cannot be measured.

Similarly, creating measurable goals makes it easy to determine if one has progressed in the direction adequately or not. So, there should be a well-thought-through plan at the Executive/

MD level for monitoring the progress. An action plan should be drawn to complete in the agreed time frame.

11.2.4   Goals should be attainable

Attainable goals stretch the limits of what one thinks is possible. Many times, we overestimate ourselves when our self-esteem is high. In business, moderation is the best option. Being too optimistic or pessimistic leads you to a place which you did not wish to be.

Goal setting requires utilising past experience and a deeper understanding of our senior leaders and that of the organisation. A goal set should be a stretch but realistic and achievable.

11.2.5   Goal should be Relevant

Many times, boards of a company are presented with innovative proposals that look attractive, but the existing company has no experience and do not make sense to experiment at that stage. They must continue to focus on improving/expanding existing lines of business.

Relevant goals focus on what is expected of the desired state.

11.2.6   Goal should be time - bound

Time-bound goals have specific deadlines. It is expected that the desired objective will be achieved before the deadline. Time-bound goals are challenging and grounding. The key is to set a deadline, work backwards, and have parts of goals to be achieved in each particular time frame. It requires meticulous planning and close monitoring so that the project is moving as per the time schedule.

Chapter-12

Impact of Mindfulness at Work Place

> '**Mindfulness is the practice of purposely focusing your attention on the present moment and accepting it without judgement.**'
>
> **– Jon Kabat-Zinn**

Mindfulness is a practice where you focus on being intensely aware of what you are feeling, sensing without making a judgement. It is very important for day-to-day operations in the place of work.

Mind management is a challenge for most of us. Its origin could be internal or external. But once you have learnt to be aware, it brings clarity to our thought process.

While negative mode leads us in a rigid way of thinking, perceiving, and acting, whereas awareness allows flexibility. We can gather information fully, understand it from many angles, and respond as needed rather than in a particular inflexible, preconceived fashion. In the grip of the negative mode, our thoughts and feelings rush to a conclusion, giving us little choice over what we think, feel, or do. But when we are aware, we open the way to more inner freedom of choices. The impressions of the steps we have taken on the path of confusion gradually disappear in the shifting sands. (Ref. 2)

When we catch a negative mood starting to take hold, sometimes all our minds need is a gentle reminder that we are caught in a downward spiral. This kind of "remind-fulness" seems more important in these situations of distracted multitasking. Amidst the inner clutter, we can easily slip into a negative mood without possessing adequate knowledge. This can be quite infectious and can quickly get passed on to the team.

2. Mindfulness operates as the mind's monitor in spotting a problem and applying an appropriate remedy. It gives us the inner space from which to calibrate what we need in the moment.

3. A mindful awareness can be seen as a mode director. From the mindful perspective, as we become more mindfully present, we are creating what amounts to an inner secure base - one that does not depend on someone else to help us but rather one, we generate from within. This can provide a positive view of looking at the world.

4. We never know what the next moment is going to be. It is always something new, the function of being mindful is that whatever happens, you are aware of what is happening in that moment. There's no real objective to mindfulness beyond just being aware of whatever it is." (Ref-2)

Mindfulness Works as

12.1 knowing awareness that observes the causes of a problem

12.2 an intuitive awareness that observes the causes of problems and knows the apt solution.

Example:

When we wanted to reduce credit days in the Paints business, there was a general awareness of the need, but internally, we were all fearful. There was no way to gauge which way it was going to turn out. The inner self was clear that it must be done if the business was to survive. Finally, it was done despite many disagreements. During that period, interest rates was above 10%, and we saved on that interest payment, thus improving our bottom line. Mindfulness brings everything into balance on its own.

Chapter-13

Understanding of the Mindset

Research has shown that the view you adopt for yourself deeply affects the way you lead your life. It can determine whether you become the person you want to be and whether you accomplish the things you value. It is very crucial because this reflects who you are. At the workplace, it is important to be able to inspire people to take on challenges, have perseverance until the task is completed.

I have used this growth vs. Static mindset concept in many businesses and mentored senior leaders to practice. This provides you clear space at the time of major decision-making. The decisions which are crucial for the organisation. An example was when a senior salesperson advised me not to go for investment in a paint's unit. I heard him patiently and reached my own conclusion after analysing the merit of his presentation. A detailed discussion is given below as it is complex, and we need to have a clear understanding of this concept.

Mindset can be generally described as a growth mindset or a fixed mindset. The growth mindset is based on the belief that your basic qualities are things you can cultivate through your efforts. People may differ in their initial talents, aptitudes, interests, or temperaments, but each one of them, willing to learn, can change and grow through application and experience. Most of the successful leaders have a growth mindset, and some who are on the borderline can move by putting efforts to acquire this competency.

We interviewed a lot of candidates, and during those 45-minute sessions, we could establish whether the candidate belonged to a static or growth mindset. We also looked at the behavioural part and found the growth mindset was the one to select.

A fixed mindset is rigid in its practices and unwilling to explore, which has a risk component. For them, 'Nothing ventured, nothing gained' is not worth it. Exploration and innovation are rarely their strengths.

Risk and effort are two things that might reveal inadequacies of a fixed mindset and show that you were not up to the task. In fact, it's surprising to see that people with the "fixed mindset do not believe in effort."

Growth Mindset

Growth mindset people are continuously trying to improve. They surround themselves with the most able people they can find. They look at their mistakes and deficiencies squarely and ask what skills they will need, and what the company will need in the future. Because of this, they can move forward with confidence. This is the process of continuous learning, and I am one of its practitioners.

That is based on facts and not fantasies. Most of the successful people belong to this group. I, myself, have learnt to be in that state most of the time and succeeded in achieving our goals.

Growth mindset people focus on development, ideas about meeting challenges, and are willing to put in the necessary effort. With a growth mindset, you believe you can develop yourself, then you are open to accurate information about yourself, including negative feedback.

It is interesting that those with the growth mindset seem to have that talent. For example, the team formation for the Paints business was unique. We had perseverance and did not hire anybody who did not meet the growth mindset definition.

The result was that we had an extraordinary team which delivered more than the set-out goal each year.

Jack Welch after a bad investment said-

'True self-confidence is the courage to be open, welcome change and new ideas regardless of their source. It is reflected in your mindset, your readiness to grow. He learnt over a period how to be a growth mindset, a guide and not a judge. He learnt how to hire people for their mindset not their pedigree. Originally, academic pedigree impressed him but later he changed to looking for people filled with passion and a desire to get things done.'

A growth mindset understands that important qualities can be cultivated. They learn how roadblocks to be dealt with and removed. They are aware of their physical and mental limits but also how to stretch when the situation arises.

The discovery that the brain has neuroplasticity, and a growth mindset is able to learn and manoeuvre in challenging times and moderate decision-making. In such cases, sometimes innovative ways of resolution emerge since many times old issues cannot be resolved by the old approach.

Depending on the orientation of the owner, leadership like fixed or growth mindset, the company's behaviour will be, and this percolates down to the last employee.

Example

Acquiring an autoclave in ten days, commissioning at midnight, doing a water trial followed by real conversion to a product where a different mindset focused on the goal, was an example of people with a growth mindset aligning themselves and overcoming all problems by challenging themselves and succeeding.

One can realise if the organisation has a static or growth mindset when you enter the reception. The way a visitor is treated, and the receptionist forgets to connect you to the person you had come to meet is definitely in a decline stage and can be put in the static mindset category. I have tested this with many units, and many times my decision was made after experiencing the environment.

If I look at components of mindset, it clearly leads you to connect with the value system and culture of the place. Culture is about people, and if you have a vibrant culture, the sky is the limit for growth. But if the founder unknowingly or knowingly brought in poor practices for the enterprise, it will be in a decline stage sooner than later. I have experienced many local and international units and could easily feel which ones have a future.

I have thus given a brief description of culture because when you get a chance to lead, all that latent talent you have, must blossom out.

The simple definition of the culture of an enterprise is

"This is how things are done here."

This communication extends from the behaviour of the receptionist to the manager and ultimately the workforce. Cultures emanate from the beliefs, practices, and conduct of the head of the family, owner, entrepreneur, or the Chairman of the organisation. Cultures come into being when qualities of a specific group are passed on from one generation to another. Culture represents the beliefs and behaviours of the existing organisation which new employees inducted follow automatically as they watch the behaviours around them.

Organisations that can adapt quickly to a changing environment are the ones that will survive in the long-term. An adaptive culture allows a risk-taking, trusting, and proactive approach of the organisation. Individuals support each other to identify issues and find quality solutions.

Unique is what we call the 'culture of learning'. Culture thrives on learning. A learning culture that drives everything we do at every level, every day is a bubbling crucible of ideas and learning, with people playing the roles of teacher and student. The passion to learn, obsession with finding a better way, every day. More than just an exciting, exhilarating, and fun part of analysing, improving, controlling, or locking in the process once they have found an optimum solution.

One example mentioned in the book is the doubling of the autoclave capacity in the chemical business.

Chapter-14

Explanation of Competencies

Improvements can be successfully carried out if you are an authentic leader. It takes a little time for the existing system to figure out your mindset, and then some will agree while some will resist. This negativity has to be corrected by mentoring or transfer to an area where their competencies match.

From Business Planning to strategy formation and management of different functions were discussed earlier. Now we have covered self-awareness, mindset and its impact on culture. If you gradually acquire these learnings, you are on your way to be a fearless successful leader.

One area which is not much focused, but I have used fruitfully in the book is - **competencies**.

I have coached/mentored in most of my assignments and recommend learners to understand competencies in order to grow. I have used these competencies frequently in my professional as well as in personal life. It is used in the book, and it is important to understand its meaning and significance.

In the area of competencies, there is a lot of work done by Daniel Goleman on EQ (1998), which primarily prescribed personal and social competencies (with twenty-five subsets) that have not been covered here.

In 2011, Edward J. Gripe and Richard S. Mansfield defined three groups - competencies dealing with people, business, and self-management (with thirty-one subsets - Ref-6). I have selected the ones which are used more often for success.

Competence is what one does well when compared to others. Competence is a combination of demonstrable characteristics that enable and improve the efficiency of the performance of a task. It is a combination of skill, knowledge, and behaviour.

There are many analyses done on this subject, but we have discussed the ones I have used or learnt during this period. The importance of this is that at different levels of work (Ref. 6), different competencies are required. This helps us to decide at an interview between the competencies the candidate demonstrates vs. the requirement of the job. Similarly, in reorganisation, you can have a competency-based organisation. These are used in the journey and its obvious importance.

Important competencies

14.1   LEARNING

> **'I don't divide the world into the weak and strong or the success and the failures. I divide the world between Learners and Non-learners.'**
>
> **– Benjamin Barber - an eminent sociologist**

The process rather than the content or the results is more exciting. One is energised by the steady and deliberate journey from ignorance to competence. The excitement leads you to undertake adult learning experiences. The outcome of the learning is less significant than 'getting there'.

In a work situation, the individual-

a)   Quickly understands a new situation/task

b)   Easily learns new information regarding changing products, operations, and the new environment

c)   It is open to and understands new concepts

Robert Sternberg, the present-day guru of intelligence, writes that the major factor in whether people achieve expertise **'is not some fixed prior ability, but continuous learning and hard work.'**

Learning is never ending, so one should allocate some part of their time schedule to learn 'one thing' every day. This is one reason practising every day increases your chances to grow better in personal as well as professional life.

14.2   HARD WORK

'Nothing worthwhile comes early. Half effort does not produce half results. It produces no results; continuously work and hard work is the only way to accomplish results that last.'

– Hamilton Holt - American author

A static mindset believes that nothing comes out of hard work. They believe they are 'smart' so need not put in that much effort as individuals who are not that smart. I am not aware of any leader who has reached the top management level working 9 to 5. Nothing ever comes to one that is worth having, except because of hard work.

Effort is the key. Success is seen as a result of effort and practice and not just innate talent. Innate talent, if not put in adequate hard work, is unlikely to succeed.

14.3   RESPONSIBILITY

'If you are working on something you care about, you don't need to be pushed. The vision pulls you.'

– Steve Jobs

It is an internal commitment to deliver the promise you made by taking that responsibility. There could be roadblocks on the way, and it becomes your responsibility to clear them. You cannot afford to fail because you will not be able to live with your inner self if not discharged. Apologies are not enough. Excuses and rationalisation are unacceptable.

Once work is completed, you shall be known as a person who can be trusted to deliver. Whenever a challenging task comes up, you shall be at the top of the mind of decision-makers. It is a commitment that will not accept any excuses for failure.

14.4   ADAPTABILITY

> 'It is not the strongest of the species that survives, nor the most intelligent that survives.
> It is the one that is most adaptable to change.'
>
> – Charles Darwin

This is the ability to interact with people from different disciplines and backgrounds. In other words, it is about coping with sudden or unknown challenges. The temperament has to be such that it can handle ambiguities and come up with appropriate solutions. It is about both challenges at work and dealing with different people at different levels suitably.

14.5 INTEGRITY

'If you do not have integrity, you have nothing. You can't buy it. You can have all the money in the world, but if you are not a moral and ethical person, you really have nothing.'

– Henry Kravis

Integrity is the quality of being honest and having strong moral principles. There are hidden compulsions which surface when you are faced with something valuable, especially when you are alone. Your internal value system comes into play to concede to greed or your moral values which guide not to indulge. Integrity is about the practice of maintaining ethical standards, honesty, and consistency in action. It is the internal compass of an individual to decide what is right and what is not right.

An authentic leader must display high ethical standards and honesty at work and be seen to be believed. Integrity builds trust and is reassuring to the workforce.

Poor integrity is common, especially in financial or technical documentation. Fudging results is a big temptation. In the Pharma industry, the FDA found many such incidences during audits. There are strict systems in place; despite that, certain individuals are able to beat the system.

Good leadership is about holding high moral values and resolution, never succumbing to temptations. Integrity, thus, is about the alignment of vision, values, systems, and procedures and is seen to be a consistent behaviour.

14.6   SELF-DISCIPLINE

> **'Self-discipline begins with the mastery of your thoughts.**
> **If you do not control what you think, you can't control what you do.'**
>
> **– Napoleon Hill**

In today's industrial environment, it is crucial to understand the thinking and emotions of the people who are responsible for yielding outstanding results.

In this context, we need to have some background on how our thinking, i.e. how communication, decision-making, and problem solving are processed through different parts of our brain.

These parts work through three components of our thinking-

- primal,
- emotional and
- logical.

Decision-making centres are at different locations.

a) The oldest part is the primal brain concerned with threats and survival to cater to sudden challenges.
b) Limbic system or emotional brain, responsible for our emotions, coordination of movement, likes and dislikes, pleasure and pain.
c) Prefrontal cortex.

The rational brain can discern between right and wrong, good or bad, decision-making, being aware of consequences, and problem solving. This part, if understood and practised, can bring in desired behaviour and can manage primal as well as emotional brains. This balance, once achieved, will be the differentiator between a leader and a follower.

> **'Self-discipline is a form of freedom. Freedom from laziness and lethargy, freedom from expectations and demands of others, freedom from weakness and fear and doubt, self-discipline allows a person to feel his individuality, his inner strength, his talent. He is master of rather than a slave to his thoughts and emotions.'**
>
> **– Harvey Dorman**

Self-discipline allows you to do what you want to do and focus on the most important aspect in your 'to-do' list.

It is the superpower of focus in a world of distractions, allowing you to overcome procrastination, excuses, bad habits, low motivation, failures, and self-doubt.

You must channelise your habits aligned to your goal and values by increasing your self-awareness and self-discipline. Once it is a habit, you need less self-control and self-awareness, and you are on your way to cement your values and goals in your mindset and among the coworkers.

The key is that one should be aware of their strengths and respect oneself for those characteristics. This awareness guides our behaviour inside and outside the environment.

Self-discipline has been very crucial in my growth. It was a kind of a value system that was passed on to us through the behaviour of our parents. It can also be acquired.

Successful people are known to be highly disciplined and achieve near-impossible targets because of their well organised thought process.

Self-Discipline is about the power to manage your thoughts, emotions, and thereby behaviour. It is about letting go of small pleasures for better living, having a fully engaged life, expressing your potential, and finding fulfilment.

Self-discipline is the most essential skill for you to achieve your personal or professional goals in life. It is the master of all virtues, the engine of all growth, and the compass you need to live in accordance with your highest goal and values day after day.

The time you spend mastering it will pay you rich dividends. Develop self-discipline for the right reasons like pursuing your goal.

True self-control means moderation, a balance and not just in what we do but also in how we think, how we feel, how we conduct ourselves, work vs. other activities which you face in a world of chaos and confusion.

People with good self-discipline are healthier, happier, and more successful than others in the journey of life. (ref-12)

> **'Most powerful is he who has himself in his own power.'**
>
> **– Seneca, Epistles**

14.7   PERSEVERANCE

> **'Our greatest weakness lies in giving up. The most certain way to succeed is always to try just one more time.'**
>
> **– Thomas A. Edison**

It is the quality of continuing to try to achieve a goal despite facing difficulties or delays. It involves persistence, steadfastness in pursuing a goal despite several roadblocks coming in the way.

Researchers find a lot of difficulties prior to making a discovery and need perseverance to achieve their set-out objectives. I have experienced that giving up is easy. For example, a new product required to complete the product range was started and abandoned after the first experiment as the gland of the autoclave leaked. The scientist was working on another project and his whole focus shifted to that project.

When I came as a manager, I looked at the progress of all the projects. The one which was left out since the first experiment had failed, discussed with a chemist and asked to test if the equipment is in good condition. Once it was approved by engineering, the experiment was initiated. The experiment turned out to be positive, except that the conversion of raw material to the desired product was on the lower side. We continued vigorously to optimise the process and in about eight months were ready for scale up trials. We need to have perseverance to overcome obstacles.

Perseverance is a competency to continue striving towards a goal despite roadblocks. It enhances skills, confidence, resilience, and inspires the team.

14.8 THINKING COMPETENCIES

There are four thinking competencies used by management, and based on these, when demonstrated in a working environment, a mix of one or the other competencies is used. These also help to decide the level of work and are a key input for reorganisation.

Mainly three key competencies have been worked out-

14.8.1 Analytical

Thinking involves looking for underlying causes, thinking through the consequences of different courses of actions and developing clear criteria for making decisions. It is about deduction, drawing logical conclusions from the available data.

14.8.2 Strategic

This involves consideration of the future needs of businesses, departments, and organisations, thinking about present policies, processes, and methods which might be affected gradually by future developments and trends. To develop long-term goals and strategies considering the long-term ramifications.

14.8.3 Innovativeness

Thinks in terms of options when identifying solutions and is original alternatives to conventional thinking. For example, generating original and imaginative ideas for the development of new products or upgrading the existing ones.

> **'I never dreamed about success. I worked for it.'**
>
> **– Estée Lauder**

It is a powerful reminder that success often comes from a growth mindset and hard work rather than just dreaming about it.

References

1. The Power of learning by Emily Smith-page 84-85 Penguin Random House LLC New York
2. Mind Whispering-Tara Bennett Goleman-Harper Collins Publishers
3. Good to Great-Jim Collins Page-121, 142 Harper Collins Publishers
4. Mindset-Dr Carol Dweck Constable and Robinson Ltd, U.K.
5. Discipline is Destiny-Ryan Holiday Penguin Random House LLC, USA
6. Break Free and Grow-Param Bhargava Ph.D.
7. Mindful Self-Discipline-Giovanni Dienst Mann
8. Change the Culture-Roger Connors and Tom Smith Penguin Group, USA page 25, 27
9. The Strategic Leaders Roadmap - Harbir Singh and Michael Useem Wharton School Press
10. Strengths Finder 2.0 by Tom Rath-Gallup Press: Page 113
11. The Truth about Leadership by James M. Kouzes & Barry Z. Posner
12. Corporate culture and Performance-John P Kotter and James L Heskett page 11. The Free Press, New York